How You Can Be an

Awesome
Grandpa

How You Can Be an

Awesome
Grandpa

James Gooch

iUniverse®

HOW YOU CAN BE AN AWESOME GRANDPA

iUniverse books may be ordered through booksellers or by contacting:

iUniverse LLC
1663 Liberty Drive
Bloomington, IN 47403
www.iuniverse.com
1-800-Authors (1-800-288-4677)

ISBN: 978-1-4917-3139-0 (sc)
ISBN: 978-1-4917-3140-6 (hc)
ISBN: 978-1-4917-3141-3 (e)

Library of Congress Control Number: 2014907083

Printed in the United States of America.

iUniverse rev. date: 09/26/2014

Contents

Introduction

Any man can be a grandfather, but it takes someone special to be *Grandpa.*

This book was written to help grandfathers be great, wonderful, and unforgettable. It started out as information just for me, and then I realized it needed to be shared with others. Even though I compiled the data and wrote the book, I am constantly referring back to it to refresh my awareness of the best ways to interact with my children and grandchildren. Since I will forget things now and then, it is especially nice to have a written resource to remind me.

I found it interesting when I let a few trusted friends read the manuscript, that even many of the grandmothers were gathering thoughts and useful gems of information for their own reference. I was surprised at the positive responses I received from these readers, for it truly is a useful resource for all ages of moms and dads, grandpas and grandmas.

Being a parent can be the most frustrating and rewarding experience one can have. When children come into our lives, they can bring so much disruption, turmoil, stress, and noise, at times one can hardly stand it. Yet when they leave, the silence can be unbearable. Our greatest moments of happiness often are directly related to our children. Life's knowledge does not come easy or without sacrifice, especially when it relates to children.

As our lives continue to move forward, we have an additional opportunity to experience the joy of grandchildren. Being a grandparent can bring much happiness, and as the saying goes, *happiness is the destination, but it's also the path.*

To help with this opportunity I have put together a collection of ideas, suggestions, techniques, experiences, and thoughts shared with me by both grandfathers and grandchildren, which, if followed, will make your experience as a grandpa more rewarding and successful. After applying these techniques you too will hear comments such as, "Grandpa, you are the best grandpa in the whole world."

Please note, when referring to Grandpa G, I am speaking of the almost perfect grandpa. He seemed to always have the right answer or story for every situation. He was funny, nonjudgmental, compassionate, and understanding. Everyone liked being around Grandpa G. He always seemed to know what to say, how to say it, and, most importantly, at the right time. However, he is not one person. Grandpa G is compiled from a whole host of respected grandpas who contributed to the surveys and interviews. I have found, by emulating the advice from these different grandpas, that I have become a much better grandpa to my own children and grandchildren and am coming closer to the Grandpa G model.

Chapter 1

I Am a Grandpa—Now What?

I remember as if it were yesterday, nervously sitting in that hospital room, anxiously waiting, lost in deep thought, switching back and forth with excitement and fear. I was going to be a father. My mind racing, *I am going to be a father, how cool,* then . . . *oh no, I am going to be a father; I'm not prepared for this; how am I going raise a child? I am too young. How am I going to teach the child what to do? I don't have the wisdom my dad did. I don't make enough money; how am I going to pay for college?* The waiting seemed to go on forever.

Then more panic, more questions: *What if something goes wrong with the baby or, worse, my wife; how will I survive? I don't know anything about babies, I don't even know how to change a diaper . . .* Then the pleading prayer phase: *Please, Lord, don't let anything happen to my wife or the baby.*

Switching again: *Will it be a boy or girl? It doesn't matter as long as the baby is healthy.* Pondering: *Why do people always say that? Because deep down, every man wants a boy, and every woman wants a girl. I guess we say it to be politically correct or to not offend our child, but secretly we are hoping for one gender over the other.* Nervously, I paced with thoughts randomly switching back again: *Just think! I am going to be a father!* So the melodrama of thoughts and emotion continued with panic, hope, and anticipation, waiting for news. I believe I had every scenario possible, with endless imaginable outcomes. They were all charging through my mind as I waited in the hospital room.

Trying anything in the long process of waiting, hoping to distract my mind, I would pace up and down the hallways. Do you know, the old Good Samaritan Hospital had 255 twelve-inch square tiles from the waiting room to the entryway, with twenty-three overhead light fixtures? I know; I counted them all several times.

While I was in this state of insecurity and heavy self-evaluation, the nurse came in to take me back to see my beautiful, radiant, tired wife. Did I say beautiful? She just glowed with a special elegance that lighted her whole being, and it just overpowered me. While caught up being near her, an overwhelming feeling of relief and love filled my soul when I saw she was okay. The nurse then gently pulled me away to show me this wrinkly, tiny bundle wrapped in a pink blanket, with a pink beanie on her head, with pink socks on her tiny feet, in a pink basket.

Relying on my noted pattern of observation, I proceeded to ask, "Is it a boy?" It just seems I always miss the obvious. Thank goodness for her understanding mother.

Looking back at my wonderful wife, for she never looked more magnificent than at that moment, and seeing her questioning look as she waited for a word of approval, I said, holding this little girl, "She is the most beautiful thing I have ever seen." I fell in love with her from the moment I saw her, and that love has never left for all these years and never will.

Now twenty-four years later, my sweet little bundle is on a gurney heading for the delivery room to have her first child. The same old worries, images, and concerns come back to me. *She is too young to be a mother.* The pacing, the long waiting, the excitement, and the worry all begin again.

Do you know, the new Samaritan Hospital has 290 twelve-inch square tiles between the waiting room and the entry door, with thirty-two overhead light fixtures? As I was pacing, it hit me: *I am going to be a grandfather! Wait, I am too young to be a grandfather. I don't have the wisdom of my father . . .* While in this familiar state of confusion, my son-in-law came to get me, and I was taken into the small delivery room, where my beautiful daughter was holding the most precious bundle I had ever seen. It was wrapped in a pink blanket, with a pink beanie, pink socks, in a pink basket, and, of course, I asked, "Is it a boy?"

Grandma just rolled her eyes and muttered, "Oh brother." It is good to know that some things never change, no matter how old we get.

Now that I was a grandfather, I wanted to be the best grandfather I could be. If I was going to be the most terrific grandfather, then I needed to learn as much as possible. Aha! Another project was born. But this one was going to be my passion. Like many other projects, I figured it should be easy: I would just find a book somewhere, rent a movie, and have all the information I desired. With all the confidence in the world, I figured if I put aside a whole day, I could find everything I wanted. What was I thinking?

Monday morning, I headed for the library. I stopped at the front desk and asked a nice lady at the information desk where I could find a book about grandfathers.

She said, "Those would be in the children's section."

I responded, "No, I don't want a children's book, but one written for adults, *like grandfathers.*"

"Oh, we do have some written about the childhood experiences—mostly by women telling of their experience with their grandfathers," she said.

"Do you have any written by grandfathers?" I asked.

"No, but we do have several written for grandmothers. Will that help?" she asked.

"Not really. I am looking for reference material to help me be a better grandfather," I said.

"We don't have any books just for grandfathers, but we do have several for fathers—it is the same thing, isn't it? After all, kids are kids, right?" she answered.

I just looked at her, and then I said, "You don't have any children, do you?"

"No, I do not. Why do you ask?" she said.

"No reason," I said as I walked away, thinking she didn't have a clue.

So the search began to find any information referring to grandfathers. It was like looking for water in the desert. There isn't much available. I looked in libraries, the Internet, bookstores, and even school courses. Nothing was there. The librarian was right, however; I did find several references for fathers and grandmothers. As it turned out, what I thought would be a one-day project became several days, then one week, then two months. After two months, I had completely depleted all of my creditable resources. I realized there is no easily found information available for grandfathers.

One day, while explaining my dilemma to one of my close friends, he—being a grandfather—started telling me about his experiences with his grandchildren. Since he had several grandchildren, he had what I thought was a wealth of knowledge. Right then, I had an epiphany. It was like being hit with a hammer. The lightbulb came on: maybe I could start asking people about their experiences, good and bad, as a grandfather. Then an additional thought came: *why not ask more questions of people of all ages concerning their own grandfathers, from their perspective as a grandchild?* To test my idea, I thought I would begin by asking people about their relationships with their own grandfathers.

The next day, I started my quest of questioning people about what they remembered about their own grandfathers. The response was amazing. Every single person had something to say. I had really stumbled onto something. I quickly realized I needed to put together a formal questionnaire to get the answers I required. The questionnaire needed to be expansive enough to include questions for grandchildren about their grandfathers and questions for grandfathers about being one.

Before I knew it, I had launched an extensive survey, seeking answers from a little over four hundred folks responding to questions about grandfathers. It amazed me that from the original concept of gathering information to help me be a better grandfather, it had turned into this major project. Expanding from the scheme of a one-day visit to the library to a compilation of all this personal information, it would be far more valuable than what someone would have put in a single source like a book.

The only negative responses, for the most part, were from those unfortunate individuals who couldn't remember their grandfathers because they had passed away while they were young or before they were born. For them, there was a feeling of great and deep loss in their lives as they described how much they wished they had known their grandfathers.

Thank goodness grandparents live much longer today than in years past. Many will live long enough to see not only their own children grow to adulthood but their grandchildren as well. In our modern world, more seniors live longer and will be available to develop relationships and interact with their own grandchildren and children. In the last twenty years, the life expectancy of men and women has extended by ten to twenty years due to advancements in the world of medicine.

There is no doubt that grandmothers, mothers, girlfriends, and wives have a big influence on our thinking, but this is about grandfathers relating to their grandchildren. So I have not included the information gathered about grandmothers, which was often included in the interviews.

Chapter 2

The Interviews and Results

Thinking of Grandpa makes me smile. I will always hold my cherished memories of him close to me, for someday he might not be around anymore.

—Survey respondent

As I began to talk to grandfathers, my questions were very simple—I was only asking for advice about their successes and failures and about their relationships with their grandchildren. The simple questions resulted in simple answers. It quickly became apparent I needed to delve deeper to elicit more specific information. I had the idea that individuals could fill out a questionnaire. However, it didn't work as I had imagined. People just didn't write down their thoughts and feelings. The large blank spots on the paper made me realize this information had to be gathered by one-on-one interviews in a question-and-*listen* format.

After many conversations, I started to expand the questions to an even larger, more extensive survey. I surveyed old and young grandfathers from different socioeconomic levels in North America. Their backgrounds encompassed all sorts of life experiences in careers, family structures, religions, and personal lifestyles. The interviews included several hundred people and were conducted over a three-year period.

Because of the overwhelming results, I decided to include not just grandfathers but basically all individuals who were willing to answer questions relating to what they remembered about their experiences with their grandfathers. These interviews, generated from grandfathers and grandchildren, brought to light very revealing stories and often very moving and cherished memories. It turned out to be much more rewarding and revealing as it unfolded than I could ever have expected or imagined.

During the interviews, I noticed a marked difference between how individuals responded to the questions about their own grandfathers and how grandfathers talked about being a grandfather. When individuals reflected on memories of being a grandchild, they were more open and free-flowing with their thoughts and emotions, probably because the childhood memories didn't have any responsibilities attached to them. But when I questioned a grandfather about his role as a grandfather, his response would be much more fraught with a feeling of accountability. It wasn't easy-going, but carefully put forth with thought, logic, and reasoning, much like a teacher to a student.

The thing that fascinated me the most was the manner in which individuals who talked about their relationships with their grandfathers began their responses. It didn't matter the setting or situation—in public, by ourselves, busy, relaxed, cold, or hot—when I asked the first question, they would pause; then a noticeable relaxing of their body took place, almost if they were moving into another state of existence as their mind and spirit began gathering significant moments from their past, searching for a way to convey their emotions about those choice experiences of their younger lives. You could actually see in their eyes a special light emitting from them as they described their experiences with their grandfather or grandfathers. For a moment, you could see their thoughts and feelings of happiness while they reflected back in time.

As they described each of their experiences or stories, I couldn't help being drawn into and captured by their wave of feelings. The feelings were real, deep, and powerful. They wanted to share the ups and downs, the happiness and sadness, the laughter, the pain, all of it coming forth in great detail with wonderfully animated expressions of their joy in being able to reveal these stories about their ancestors. It was also enlightening to me that, *in almost every interview, there was a touching expression of love and reverent respect for their grandfathers.*

Unfortunately, I do admit there were a few who didn't have good experiences or specific, positive occurrences relating to their grandfather. Their experiences were among the sad or disappointing aspects of life. Some told of terrible trials in their young lives. I have decided to not focus on those, for they were few and beyond the scope of this book.

As I continued gathering information from the questions, the results continued to grow even more. I never got tired of listening to these stories. This was mainly due to the wide range and variety of responses and details that emerged from almost all the respondents. It seemed they wanted to share everything with me. The questions and responses became more about feelings and emotions than deeds and activities. Each had a story they had to share, each one led to another and then another.

Yet I had so many questions that needed to be answered.

Renewing the search, I started to notice common experiences that were held at a higher level of happy memory. I noticed some experiences survived the test of time, while others were erased, the details lost. I started to ask myself questions:

- Why did individuals remember one event with their grandfather over another?
- What were the common denominators?
- Why did one activity create a cherished memory, while another was lost in obscurity?
- How is a relationship with a grandchild different from that with your own child?
- Why is one grandfather more remembered than another?
- Why is one grandfather loved more than another?

- How does one become not just a good grandfather, but a great one?
- What traps do grandfathers fall into when talking to grandchildren?
- How does a grandfather's role fit into the family structure?
- What can I do to become a better grandfather?
- How can I become an *awesome* grandpa?

While pondering these questions, I realized most of the answers could be found in the interviews. I decided to assemble the information into some manner of order. The results were amazing. They formed a blueprint that could help anybody to be a better grandfather.

I noticed there were several desired features, attributes, or characteristics about Grandpa requested by grandchildren. The following list is just a quick general snapshot of the attributes. Understand, at this point, I am not going into too much detail on each relationship trait for now, but will give you a quick idea of some of the suggestions needed to develop the fantastic relationship that we all want and need with our grandchildren. In the following chapters, I will go into a much deeper explanation of the desired characteristics.

Heritage

The first requested feature was that children wanted to know about their heritage. For this reason, it is important to have good relationships between grandchildren and grandfathers, to help them discover who they are and why they act or look a certain way. Everyone has this desire and longing for answers from their grandparents.

Relationships between a grandfather and a grandchild can and will have a far-reaching effect for many generations. Children always want to know about who and where they came from. One of the biggest websites on the Internet is designed to help people track information about their ancestors. It is often overwhelmed with people searching for information about their heritage. The need to know who we are is deeply ingrained in all of humankind.

One granddaughter had asked her grandpa a question about herself. "Grandpa, I love mint chocolate; do you know where that came from?"

Grandpa answered, "Yes, your grandmother loves mint chocolate too. I am sure you inherited it from her."

The young girl responded, "Great, now I know who I get that from: Grandma!"

For years, she told everyone she loved mint chocolate just like her grandmother, *because her grandfather had told her so.*

Each relationship in a young child's world is unique. The grandchildren are still trying to understand all of the players in their world and where these players fit in the family structure. Each child will develop a sense of who he or she is and where he or she came from through these family relationships. That is why each child deserves the right to have a connection to all the adults in the family formation.

Quality Time

The second request was having prime, personal time together. I learned that every single grandparent wished they had more time with the grandchildren. For the children, it was to *have spent* more time with their grandfathers when they were alive. This was even true of adults reflecting back to when they were children. As I listened to their answers, not one grandfather said he wished he had spent more time at the office or playing golf. The number one regret mentioned was not being able to see or spend more time with their little grandkids.

I noticed how those grandfathers who had made a point of developing time to spend with the grandchildren were viewed as successful grandfathers whatever they did to spend time with each child. Each individual grandfather had developed his own way of establishing this special kinship. Many times it would be just doing small things together.

As one grandpa said: "Often, when with grandchildren, it would be us just sitting and talking about the details of their lives. Sharing feelings concerning day-to-day activities, their likes, dislikes, friends, spiritual thoughts, and family relationships."

Relationship

The third feature was building a good solid relationship. There is a special bond that is created with grandparents outside of normal relationships between parents and their children. It can and should be a safe zone for children to share with an adult whom they can trust, without judgment or punishment. An *unconditional-love atmosphere should exist*. There was an interesting correlation in almost all the interviews of adult children who felt they were successful in their current lives. All said they had felt loved and respected by their grandfather. Of course, this was after they got past the wrinkled skin, scary faces, age spots, and other oddities nature had imposed upon Grandpa! Being able to talk in a safe zone to a grandparent is critical for grandchildren.

One grandfather explained. "It was great just hanging out with my grandchildren. Since I didn't have to be the disciplinarian parent, I made it safe for them to say whatever came to their minds, without any judgment. Some of the subjects were amazing—from cartoon characters, family, boyfriends, school, fashion, the latest electronic games, spiritual beliefs to sports stars. We just have fun talking."

To build these safe areas, many grandfathers developed great activities with their grandchildren, helping to build quality relationships. They included working together on projects, going fishing or camping, going for walks, working on cars, playing musical instruments, exploring their singing talents together, watching sports, building something, or most often, telling stories. Children like to play. With young children, it can be playing tag or hide-and-seek. It may be just running through the house chasing each other, enjoying the screams of joy only a small child can make (much to *Grandma's* dismay). Children want to have fun. Grandfathers can provide some of that fun.

Each age and sex is different. With boys, it might be throwing a ball, shooting Nerf guns, or playing basketball. With girls, it could be the same activities or might include things like playing with dolls and tea parties. It makes sense that a one-year-old is not interested in the same enterprises as a teenager. One very wise grandfather gave me this nugget of information:

> *If you focus and direct your function toward the youngest child in the room, the others will join in and appreciate it as well.*

Another revealing truth was how the time shared with granddaughters varies greatly from the activities involved with grandsons. Each gender required different things from Grandpa. At all ages not only do girls and boys think differently, but they relate differently as well. I found grandfathers have to be sensitive to those needs and gear their dealings individually with each child. Each child wants his own time with Grandpa. For some, it may be sports-related; for others it is just reading a book together. *Remember: it isn't so much the activity, but the time you spend with them that makes it special for them.* The power of knowing she is loved, no matter what you do or say, will give a child the strength to face any foe, meet any obstacle, and overcome any difficulty.

Encompassed with the love of a grandchild is service and forgiveness. Find a way to serve them. Unselfish service is the best way to let a child know you love him. It sends a deep-rooted message: *I know Grandpa loves me. He is willing to take time to help me. I am important to him.*

We must, as grandpas, live not to be served but to serve, not to receive but to give; we must look beyond ourselves and sacrifice for our children and grandchildren.

An example provided by a grandchild illustrates how to be of service to your grandchildren:

When I was a teenager I overloaded myself with activities in school, church, family functions, music lessons, and sports. When I was assigned a major project for our school, I felt overwhelmed and depressed. The stress level was affecting everything I tried to do. My parents were unavailable because of travel and work-related requirements. Finally, I just broke down, unable to function. At that moment, Grandpa showed up at the door.

He had heard of my dilemma from my mom and volunteered to come and help me. He made some big sacrifices at work and other important activities in order to come to my rescue. He jumped right in by helping to organize, plan, and accomplish the big, school project. He saved me and became my biggest hero. It cemented our relationship. I will always remember his love for me.

Being willing to forgive a child is part of the loving process. Everyone messes up once in a while. It doesn't matter if it is a minor or major infraction, just forgive. You can't afford to hold grudges. Your time is already short. Besides, it is bad for your health. Forgiving the child allows him to forgive himself. Forgiving children gives them the strength to try again with a new start. It also brings you closer to them. It tells them that nothing is more important than your relationship and that we all make mistakes.

Maybe the most important part of building a relationship with your grandchild is learning to be kind. It never ceases to amaze me how many grandparents yell at their little grandchildren. Some of the surveys pictured a grandfather who left unhealed, terrible emotional wounds upon children's minds for their whole life caused by a thoughtless or mean grandfather. Kindness means being thoughtful, having a sympathetic nature, or just being courteous to your grandchild.

Safe Hands-On

The fourth attribute that endeared children to their grandfather included physical play or physical contact. Doing things like wrestling, tickling, swinging, and throwing children in the air were common social activities grandfathers did with younger children. With older children, the desire for physical connection was still present. Healthy physical attachment between a grandfather and a grandchild can start at the infant stage with holding, feeding, and playing with the baby.

The following is one of Grandpa G's stories:

> One time, when I was visiting my son and daughter-in-law, we were just sitting talking to each other, when all of a sudden my little two-year-old granddaughter walks in the room, carrying her blanket and bottle. She moved in between us while we continued to talk. First, she looked at Mom, then her dad, then at me. She made her decision, climbing upon my lap; she then pulled her blanket over her and began to drink her bottle. Soon she was sound asleep.
>
> It was one of the greatest experiences I have ever had with a child. It felt good holding her as she peacefully slept in my arms. She was safe there; she hadn't wanted to sleep in her bed but wanted to be held.
>
> I know if I hadn't had a good relationship with her, she never would have come to me that day and I would have missed a wonderful, treasured memory.

Positive Influence

The fifth attribute was building self-esteem. One way this can be done is through encouragement. This is so important to any relationship. Children have to see beyond themselves. If left alone, the burden of doubt, low self-worth or self-esteem can creep into their lives, especially in today's world of negativity. They need to have someone in their corner, rooting for them. In simple terms, everyone has to have someone who cares about the details of her life. Without constant outside encouragement, people will fail. Most individuals are incapable of finding this from within on a day-in-day-out basis. Grandpa, find ways to always encourage your grandchildren. Be their biggest cheerleader (without the outfit, of course).

Part of building self-worth comes from creating motivation and being energized. All of us need motivation to move forward. We have to have sparks in our lives to get us going. Like the engine in a car, nothing can turn on unless the spark plug creates the initial spark to fire up the engine. No mountain has ever been climbed without the first step. Grandchildren often require reasons to get started with any project pertaining to their life. Sometimes, you may be the one to inspire them to find that spark.

One of the most-remembered occurrences imprinted on grandchildren's minds is when their grandfather defended them. Especially when Grandpa defended them in front of their parents or other family members. As young children are developing their personal, character traits, they have to learn how to gain confidence in order to take risks, fight battles, find healthy relationships, and succeed in life. In order to gain that confidence, they must feel they are not alone, that someone has their back, so they can move forward with self-assurance. Grandpa, if you defend them one time in front of another person, this will create a lasting memory and a fierce bonding of loyalty with your grandchild. Even simply bragging about your grandchildren helps to build their confidence. They will know they are not on an island by themselves but part of a bigger group—their family, backed by Grandpa.

Sense of Humor

The sixth attribute mentioned was the use of humor. Humor is the sweet nectar that brings a child closer to you than any other thing you could do. It is the lifeblood of a great relationship between grandfather and grandchild.

Laughter makes a child feel good, that all is okay in the world. It is a healthy sense of play. There is a sensation of balance: *happiness is good*. Plus, *Grandpa is fun!*

Storytelling

The seventh attribute was storytelling. Every child remembers the stories Grandpa told. Often it was the same stories told to the grandchildren's parents by their father. These stories seem to have a life of their own. Sometimes, retold for generations. All children at any age love to hear a story, even if it is repeated many times over. Stories can bring comfort, humor, and family intimacy.

The main purpose for all of these features and attributes is to let children know they are special and someone cares about them. This is what builds and nourishes the relationship between a child and a grandfather.

Soon enough, a clearer picture of what a grandfather should be doing to create a close relationship with each of his grandchildren began to emerge. From the survey responses, I was able to understand both sides of the grandfather—grandchild connection in respect to their family association. Throughout the process of interviewing and studying the surveys, I was beginning to understand what constitutes a great grandfather. What I realized is that the center or heart of being a good grandfather comprises feelings and emotions that connect with the child. It isn't about the grandfather; it's about the memories created for those involved in the individual's life. That is what grandparenting should be all about.

But there was still much to learn if I were going to find the path to help me to be the awesome grandpa!

A blueprint was emerging. The more *successful* grandfathers had developed patterns of behavior and techniques required to be a better grandfather. The interviews and stories revealed trends and desired traits. Knowing I wasn't born with some of those natural traits, I put together an action plan to develop the desirable characteristics that would make me a better grandfather.

I began by implementing the concepts I had learned from these interviews with my own grandchildren, which brought about very satisfying success. The techniques translate to simple rules that are easy to understand and follow. By using basic logic and reasoning, becoming an awesome grandfather can be achieved. The dos and don'ts become common sense.

The characteristics described in the following chapters are priceless. I still go back and refer to them as a reference guide before I spend time with my grandchildren. They help me remember why certain things work and how to be an awesome grandfather. The stories come to mind as I find myself in similar situations giving me a guide to follow.

I have and still enjoy a tremendously wonderful time getting to know my grandchildren. There is no greater feeling then when a grandchild throws his or her arms around you and says, "You are the best grandpa in the whole world."

Because I have learned some of these techniques, I now have a treasured individual relationship with each grandchild. These relationships are much different from the relationships my grandchildren have with their own mothers and fathers. It is also interesting to note that the relationships I have with my grandchildren carry a different dynamic from the relationships I have with my children and their spouses. I will always and still greatly enjoy my children (the grandchildren's parents), but as for that special connection I have with each one of my grandchildren, it is priceless.

There is a story written in my own great-grandfather's diary about a boy who had a close relationship with his grandpa. It also made me chuckle amplifying how young minds work:

> A young boy and his grandpa had a very close relationship. The boy would often go to Grandpa to tell him his most troubling and private secrets. Swearing to never break his confidence, the grandpa soon earned the boy's trust. They became the best of buddies.

However, the young boy of seven could be very mischievous. He had a talent for always getting into trouble. Whenever something went wrong, he had a hand in it. He was a real-life Dennis the Menace. Being frustrated by the boy, his mom decided to have her minister talk to him.

The mother went to her church to talk to the minister. After talking to the frustrated mother, the minister decided he would have a meeting with the boy, and the mother sent the boy to the minister's office.

Upon entering the office, the boy saw the minister behind a large oak desk. The minister directed the boy to sit across from him. For effect, the minister just stared at the boy, without saying a word. Finally, the minister pointed his forefinger at the boy, narrowed his eyes, and asked, "Where is God?"

The boy looked under the desk, behind him, in the corners of the room, all around, shrugged, and said nothing.

To make the point, the minister asked in a louder voice, again pointing his finger at the small boy, "Where is God?"

Showing a little fear and nervousness, again the boy looked all around the room, returning his glance to the minister in muted silence, saying nothing.

A third time, in a louder, firmer voice, the minister leaned far across the desk and put his finger almost to the boy's nose, and asked, "Where is God?"

This time, in great fear, the boy panicked, scrambled for the door, and ran all the way home.

Finding his grandpa, the boy dragged him upstairs to his room, checking all around to see if anybody was listening. He finally said, "I am in *big* trouble."

Grandpa asked, "What do you mean, '*big* trouble'?"

The boy replied, "God is missing, and they think I did it!"

Grandpa just smiled.

Chapter 3

The Need of Family

Family is God's way of saying you're not alone.

—Grandpa G

Children need to feel they are part of a family. Their self-worth, personality, and personal development is greatly influenced by a family. The security of knowing somebody cares about them promotes a sense of happiness in their lives. All of us want to know we have someone who has our back, whom we can depend on even when we make mistakes. We need people to share our successes and our problems. Everyone craves to be needed, that one's life matters. Family units can provide this requirement. Families which are nontraditional, part-member, or step-member families can fulfill this basic necessity.

Even young children have a simple understanding of what constitutes family structure, though it can sometimes be confusing. Grandpa G told this story:

> I was at a family gathering when two of my three-year-old grandchildren, Nate and Aspen, came up to me asking a question.
>
> Nate asked, "Grandpa, are you my grandpa?"
>
> "Yes, I am," Grandpa G said.
>
> Aspen also asked, "Grandpa, are you my grandpa?"

"Yes, I am," Grandpa G replied.

Both looked at each other very confused.

Aspen asked, "Does that mean Grandma is both of our grandmothers?"

"Yes, she is," Grandpa G answered.

More confused looks.

Nate asked, "Is my father Aspen's father?"

"No, she has her own father," Grandpa G said.

Nate answered, "Good. I was afraid you were going to tell me she is my sister."

Family structure can be confusing, not only for young children but all of us these days.

We are living in perilous times as more and more individuals dishonor the marriage vow and delinquency rises among the youth. Divorces in the United States are up over 65 percent of total marriages; barely half of the adult population is married.[1] The number of unmarried couples living together has gone up over 400 percent during the past four decades. Children born out of wedlock are now over 53 percent. Many more children are growing up without having both parents in the home—41 percent. Most of these homes are headed by single mothers, with little or no male influence involved. In 2012, almost one of every two families with children was being maintained by one parent.[2]

Furthermore, many of the social restraints that in the past have helped to reinforce and to shore up the family are dissolving and disappearing. The time has come when only those who believe deeply and actively in the family will be able to preserve their families in the midst of the gathering evil around us. The family structure is being attacked at all levels. If grandparents—and especially grandfathers—don't become more involved with the family, many children will be lost to the perils of this world.

1　Pew Research—*Social & Demographic Trends,* Aug 1, 2013, "Marriage and Divorce."

2　Population Reference Bureau, Apr 2013, "Rising Trend of Births outside of Marriage"

In this world, much of our family acceptable behavior is being influenced by popular movies, TV, famous people, and the media. Even governments in their efforts to do good may be questioned in their results. The impact of free handouts, social biases and legislation in the name of political correctness or political power can have a far-reaching effect on the family. It is no wonder that parents and family members are at a loss when trying to understand the role of the outside influences and government in our society. The constant redefining of what is a family has caused such a nontraditional atmosphere that they would define the family out of existence. The basic need for family values and traditions can't be replaced with any of these outside influences. Bonds created through a family structure are irreplaceable.

Our generation has produced a pool of children and grandchildren who have misguided values emanating from multiple sources, which invite the thought that normal is abnormal and abnormal is normal. This manner of contemplation and action can develop into bad behavior. Unfortunately, bad-behaving adults often produce bad-behaving children, and that awful reality will not change simply by our lowering standards as to what constitutes bad behavior either in adults, youth, or children. We may not be able to change society, but we can help those in our own families, particularly with our own grandchildren.

As grandparents, we should not be taken in by the poorly designed arguments that the family unit is somehow tied to a particular phase of development in a moral society. We must resist that argument, which downplays the significance of the family and plays up the importance of viewing the world through the eyes of a selfish individual. We know the influence we have on our grandchildren can continue for many generations. We know that when things go wrong in the family, things go wrong in every other institution in society. Principles are compromised, whether it is in schools, work, religion, social settings, personal growth, or basic interaction in a relationship.

Wisdom from the world does not hold up when compared to family influences. There is nothing that can replace a family bond or family unit. Most all other forms of associations fail, often ending in hopelessness, pain, and misery. Family creates a feeling of happiness, friendship, and a normal life.

Family involves structure based on acceptable standards of behavior, especially regarding the interaction of others in the immediate and extended family. Family gives a sense of balance, something at a higher level of assurance, and well-being. It makes one feel he or she is not alone, that someone cares. A family develops a basis for one's life to pattern after when challenges come in times of despair and stress.

The decline in many of our families is occurring at a time when the nations of the world are moving into some of the most difficult times known. In no time in history has there ever been a need for the structure of a safe haven against the attacks against the family from all sides of society and worldly pressures.

Seeking worldly pursuits for materialistic treasure will not carry us, for they will be fleeting and lost without notice, leaving us wanting or longing for a more stable existence. Permissiveness will not help us through such crises. In hard times, how does one cope, or where do the fainthearted and lost turn for safety or relief? Family. It is critical in these times to have close relationships with generations of family members—grandparents, siblings, aunts, uncles, cousins, children, and grandchildren.

Our political institutions, such as federal government, state government, county commissions, and local councils cannot rescue us if our basic structure, the family, is not intact. Regulations, well-intended laws, rules, statutes, procedures, ordinances, civil codes cannot save us when there is hostility instead of love in the home. Food stamps, unemployment, or other government handouts cannot salvage us when many are no longer taught how to work or do not have the opportunity to work or the inclination, in some cases, to do so.

Police, armies, and court systems cannot safeguard us if too many people are unwilling to discipline themselves or be disciplined. Churches, neighbors, and friends have limited resources to provide protection and support for individuals.

Honor and morality start with parents and grandparents, developing relationships with their children and grandchildren. The question is how can the rising generations of children learn how to have morals and honor if grandparents and parents have dishonored themselves?

The family unit is under attack by evil designs to weaken our society. We must find a way to secure the family institution. We can't let influences of the world overpower our families. We must begin within the walls of our own homes, with our own families, to counter the attack and help the next generation of families.

In these times, it is critical that grandparents and parents use their time thoughtfully while teaching, loving, and nurturing their children and grandchildren. Finding time to engage in family activity and recreation is so important to all members of the family. You can only fail if you fail to keep trying!

We genuinely encourage help, real help, from our churches, schools, colleges, and universities, from respected men and women who care about the family. It can't be the village or tribe that raises the child, but rather the teaching and unconditional love from within the walls of family homes. We must have a clear vision in what is the right course of action, be it from God or a personal source. We cannot shirk. On us has been placed the responsibility directly where it belongs, and we must hold ourselves accountable with regard to the duties of a grandfather to teach our children and grandchildren correct principles. There is a need to walk upright before our maker, which implies there is no substitute for teaching our children by example.

From Grandpa G:

> We would be wise if we learned to really understand the heavy burdens and challenges of each member of our family. That we might effectively help in teaching, supporting, encouraging, and providing much-needed assistance. If we really understand and know those who depend upon us, we can be like the good shepherd who

knows each of his sheep. He leads, they follow. Together, we can build a trust and bond. He moves to the left, his flock moves to the left; he moves to the right, they move to the right. The good shepherd leads by example for the others to follow. There can be a high level of trust and comfort among those who follow, versus the uninspiring shepherd who rides behind the flock on his horse and lets the dogs do all the work. In the world today, we have too many dogs guiding the flocks and not enough good shepherds to lead the families.

Chapter 4

Positive Physical Connection (Hugs)

A grandpa's hug will linger long after he lets go.
—Grandpa G

Hugs can do a great amount of good—especially for children.
—Princess Diana

Children learn from touching. To young children, touching is everything. If they see something that catches their interest, they are driven to touch it. There are no value judgments, if it is dirty, messy, or valuable. Their only thought is by touching it, they can learn about it and be a part of it.

When a two-year-old granddaughter was visiting for the holidays, she saw a lollipop tree sitting on the coffee table. There were suckers of all shapes, colors, and sizes. She was told to pick one out to eat. In her desire to choose, she touched several to find the one she wanted. Her mom tried to push her hand down and told her to only touch one. Her cousin, who was almost four, touched only two in his selection process—again, told by his siblings to only touch one. The seven- and eight-year-olds would look very closely but didn't touch any except for the one they wanted.

As parents and grandparents, we can forget the necessity of touch as a learning-and-acceptance process for young children. Unfortunately, we adults have stifled our children's yearnings by enforcing commands of *don't touch*. Sometimes, this can create the effect of not being willing to venture out to explore new things, instead staying within approved boundaries. Physical touching is natural and desired. It is very powerful. It is needed and wished for by children. A baby's way of learning in this new world comes from touching all it sees. The connection of love for a newborn is felt through the human touch from another. Bonds are forever made by touching.

As individuals expressed their thoughts in the interviews, I noticed when children got older they still felt the necessity for human closeness. Touching is a form of acceptance. It is a very important requirement, especially in young children's lives, and quite frankly, it is still needed at all ages. Young men will fulfill this need by playing various physical games. With young girls (preteen), it may be holding Grandpa's hand while walking or just sitting next to him on the couch. However, the most common and still the best form of physical association comes from a simple hug.

I was once at a park where they had several booths set up from different vendors offering various services to raise money for a charity. What perked my interest was the number-one revenue-generating booth (which raised twice as much money as the second-place booth), was the one offering a hug for a dollar. There were lines up to twenty minutes long to just get a hug. The age groups represented in the line varied from young children to senior citizens. That just goes to show you that physical contact is and always will be the most powerful activity a person can experience.

> *A hug is a handshake from the heart.*
> —Author unknown

> *You can't give a hug without getting a hug.*
> —Author unknown

*A hug delights, warms and charms, which must be why
God gave us arms.*

—Author unknown

*Sometimes it's better to put love into hugs than to put it
into words.*

—Author unknown

Hugs express "I love you" without saying a word.

—Grandpa G

The need for a hug was manifested in the United States recently with events in ten cities. A world-renowned, cherubic Indian woman called simply Amma came to the United States to share love and a simple hug. Her first stop was Columbia University in New York City, and hundreds of New Yorkers came to see her. They waited in line, standing, kneeling, and sitting for hours just to receive a one-minute caress, a simple hug, with a few words of expressed love. Thousands came from every avenue of life—poor, educated, uneducated, bankers, teachers, mothers, fathers, wealthy, famous, street-wise criminals, old, young, business professionals—each in turn making their way to join in the line, patiently waiting for the special moment to receive an embrace of love.

It was the same in every city. As she would put her arms around each individual, she whispered, "My child, my child, my child . . ." softly rocking them back and forth, lightly kissing their head, "I love you, I love you, I love you." The feeling of warmth and love flowed from her embrace, encompassing the individual. A connection, a bond was felt and formed, a moment of peace being accepted, and an assurance, for a brief moment, that all will be okay fills the person's life.

Amma, meaning Mother, goes by the full name Mata Amritanandamayi. Her followers like to compare her to Mother Teresa and say she has embraced more than twenty-million people all over the world. Through love and kindness, she says, she wants to change the world. Her simple embraces have had a deep and lasting effect on people all over the world. Endless lines of people of all faiths come to receive a hug and heartfelt words of love and encouragement.

New Yorkers, people from Boston, Washington, DC, Chicago—it was the same in each of the ten cities she visited—all came seeking . . . *what?* Her only offering, a physical connection, acceptance, a moment of refuge, a simple hug, nothing more, from a woman who only shares love and tenderness. Each person came trying to capture something that seems to be absent from his or her life. It is sad so many had to turn to a stranger for something void in their lives, which should be available from their own family, an instant of affection.

The reality of touching or physical contact has produced several studies demonstrating that children who come from a loving, touching family do better in many aspects of life, including personal relationships, health, and society. We all need physical contact, but especially children.

One of the grandmothers was telling of a study done in several hospitals after World War II concerning research with orphaned newborns. It revealed some amazing results about touch. *I confirmed this with one of my nurse friends. She said it is common practice now in hospitals.* For some reason, children born in Mexico had *extremely lower death rates* among newborns than any other country in the world. They discovered that the hospitals in Mexico would hire a nanny to come in and hold the children while feeding them. In other hospitals, they would often feed them by putting their bottles against a pillow without human interaction. The newborns flourished in Mexico, while in other countries the newborns would give up and die—known as failure-to-thrive syndrome. From the conclusion of this study, many new standards have been implemented throughout the world. Maternity wards now have women in the nursery holding babies while they are feeding them, especially whenever the mother isn't available to feed them. The death rate among newborns declined greatly where this program was implemented.

There was another study that has stimulated a whole course in most nursing schools relating to the healing power of touch (the Healing Touch program, a method developed by

Janet Mentgen in 1980). The study showed if a nurse or doctor would touch the patient every time they came in the room, the patient recovered up to six times faster than those not touched. So now, each time a nurse or doctor comes into the room of a patient, they have been taught to touch a foot, head, or hand, creating a physical connection with the patient. By doing this, the patient relates better to them, which establishes a relationship and leads to faster healing. It is so simple a technique, yet it brings about such powerful results.

One of my favorite examples of the power of touch came from a waitress who would constantly receive more tips than the other servers at her restaurant. Not only did she receive more tips, but most of the time the tips were for much larger amounts. Nobody could figure it out. She was a little older than the other servers, and her looks weren't special compared to many of the younger ones. She wasn't overly friendly; she didn't provide any higher level of service than anyone else. After the perplexed owner told me about her, I began to watch what she did that might be different from the other servers. I didn't catch anything. One day, I asked her why she thought she received higher tips than anyone else. She pulled me to the side and told me she would tell me her secret only if I promised to not disclose it to anyone in the restaurant. She told me she had acquired this technique from an old friend of hers when she was much younger. Through time, she had perfected it after much practice.

Here was the secret: she would make sure she touched the diners at some point while serving them. If they were men dining alone or with other men, she would put a hand on their shoulder, resting it awhile in a friendly manner while talking to them. If it was a single woman or women together, she would do the same thing. If they were couples, she would be more subtle, gently making contact with diners by brushing their hand, arm, or shoulder, using either her hand or hip. She said she wouldn't make it obvious, for fear of jealousy by the partner. In our society, it is okay for a woman to touch others, as part of communications, but with men it isn't always the case, she said.

"What I do most male waiters can't do," she told me. "By making a physical connection, people feel comfortable with me. They don't know why they like me, but they do. Once I establish the connection, they feel closer to me and want to treat me as a friend, thus ending up with higher tips."

The practice of greeting others has a long history of learned techniques. Many nations have different acceptable greetings. They range from bear hugs to kisses, nods, and handshakes. Closer relationships produce more intimate contact, while more formal greetings dictate less physical contact. Yet all greetings do not require physical contact such as is in many of the Asian cultures in order to create a bond of communication. Still a simple handshake can have a far-reaching effect. This is why politicians and celebrities will work crowds by shaking hands— to develop a personal bond with their fans and voters. Simple contact makes people feel connected or special. For years after a handshake was made with a famous person, the receiver will cherish and hold dear their contact with that famous person. They will share the encounter every time the famous person's name is mentioned.

Another example of human-connection research was told to me by a grandfather whose grandson had participated in it. It took place at a school, which did an experiment relating to touching or making physical contact. One of the students would stop someone and ask them for directions. A couple of minutes later, another student would talk to the same person and ask them if they remembered the person who had asked them about the directions. Basically, there were two approaches while asking for directions. In the first approach the student asking for directions would make sure to keep his distance while talking to them. The second approach required the student to somehow make physical contact with the person, by arm or hand, in a nonobtrusive manner.

The results revealed interesting points. When the person who gave directions was questioned about the previous student who asked for the directions, the person could not remember anything about the first student. Many times, this *witness* could not even remember if the person seeking directions was a man or woman. But when physical contact was established (by touching an arm, a hand, a shoulder, etc.), the direction-givers not only remembered what sex the direction-seekers were, they also remembered things like hair color, the color of a shirt or blouse, how tall the person was, the eyes, tattoos, even down to the smallest detail. The experiment showed that physical contact allows your mind—and possibly your spirit—to lock on to the other person, creating a more thorough attachment.

In a grandpa and grandchild relationship, if contact with hugs, or simple touching takes place, a healthy bond is created between the two. A feeling of acceptance and closeness will be there.

On the reverse side, studies have shown that individuals who came from nontouching families have a different outlook on life. These individuals often were the ones who didn't fit well in society, couldn't maintain good relationships, and had poorer health. Many were involved with criminal activities at young ages.

People as a whole desire and need physical touching, whether it is a hug, holding hands, or just sitting next to someone. *Children especially want to be held. It provides comfort to them. It means all is well in their world.*

The bottom line is, if you are a grandfather who doesn't know how to bridge the gap of physically touching in a healthy way with your grandchild, then I have two words: *learn how!*

Chapter 5

The Power of the Words I Love You

The words I Love You *can soften my heart like the purr of
a kitten.*

—Grandpa G

It begins with simply telling your children and grandchildren
"I love you." When was the last time you told those closest to
you that you love them? We all know we are supposed to tell
them. We know it feels good when someone tells us they love
us. But we don't always do what we should do. For many men,
using the *love* word makes them feel awkward, unsure, and
embarrassed.

Saying I love you is only part of it. We need to say it *and
mean it.* We need to say it and show it . . . continually. Love
from us needs to be expressed and demonstrated, until they
feel it.

Unfortunately, we often assume those around us already
know how much we love them. They *must*, right? No, we should
never assume anything: make your love crystal clear to them.
There is no regret more expressed throughout history than not
telling someone you loved them. It must never be omitted in
your relationship with a grandchild and others who mean so
much to you.

In one of the interviews, a man reflected on his relationship with his grandfather and said, "I really don't know if my grandfather truly loved me, because he never said it to me. He went to my games, taught me how to fish, watched sports with me, and spent time talking to me, but not once did he say 'I love you.' I think he loved me, but I still wonder. Maybe, he was so proper all the time it just wasn't in his nature to express love through words."

From the grandfather's side, one grandfather explained why he didn't verbally express in words his love for his family: "I just assumed they knew I loved them, because I did so many things for them. It wasn't until my little granddaughter asked me why I never said 'I love you' to her that I realized my mistake."

Doing is not saying. Everyone wants to hear the words and it feels right.

One woman in her early thirties told me about an experience with her grandfather. Her grandfather was a nontalker. He hardly ever spoke. His children referred to him as Silent Dad. He would just nod when people were talking around him, hardly ever contributing to conversations. He had basically a nonverbal relationship with his children. Yet he worked hard to provide and take care of his children. He went to all their activities, giving plenty of moral support. The problem was he just didn't talk to them.

As grandchildren were brought into the family, he continued with this nonengagement pattern in his relationships with his grandchildren. His wife did all the talking, organizing, planning activities, and controlling all functions of the family. None of his children or grandchildren felt close to him, nor he to them.

The granddaughter said:

> We had moved away from the East Coast where my grandparents lived, and I hadn't seen Grandpa for some time. I decided to take a trip and visit them. While there, we were all talking, and Grandpa was doing what he

always did—being Silent Dad—just sitting there nodding. I determined it was a time for a change.

I sat right down in front of Grandpa and looked him in the eye, not letting him look away. I then said to him, "Grandpa, I want you to know how much you mean to me. I missed you so much when we moved away. Grandpa, I love you more than you will ever know."

Grandpa looked back at me, and his eyes began to water up, openly crying with tears running down his cheeks, and he said, "Tammy, I missed you too, and I love you so much. You are such a joy in my life."

The whole room went silent, with jaws dropping in shock, all staring at him. I had never known him to express any emotion before that moment; nor did anyone else in the family.

I never realized how much power was in those three words *I love you*. I think the other members of the family just didn't express them to him or each other. They had developed a shield against emotional connection through the years.

Ever since then, I had a fun and close relationship with Grandpa. For myself, I have learned to take every opportunity to say I love you to each member of my own family. What a difference it makes, bringing us all closer together.

As Grandpa G says, "If you don't tell them you love them, how will they know? Because nobody else can tell them for you."

I suggest you don't wait another minute and start contacting all those who are important in your life. Tell them you love them and why. Don't have any regrets, don't delay. Just do it. You will be surprised by the response.

Chapter 6

Unconditional Love

The love of a grandfather should not be a pretend love. It is not a greeting-card love. It is not the kind of love that is praised in popular music and movies.

> *Grandpa's love can change a child's character. It can remove anger and hatred. It can bring healing to emotional wounds of resentment and bitterness. It can work miracles.*
>
> —Grandpa G

Now how do we show unconditional love?

I asked Grandpa G how he shows unconditional love. He said,

> I start when they are young, with a game of sorts. Every once in a while, I will walk up to a child from out of the blue and just say it: "I don't care what you say, I still love you." The startled child starts to say something in return, and I'll cut him off and say, "No, I don't care what you say; I still love you"; then I start laughing.
>
> The child now understands it as a game and will continue to try to say something, trying to overtalk me,

but I will continue to cut him off with, "No, I don't care
what you say; I still love you." This will go on for several
minutes, with the stuttering child loving the attention
and the message. It is a very subtle and fun way to
convey that I will love him always, no matter what.

He is right. I tried it with my grandchildren, and they love
it, except I added, I don't care what you say or do; I still love
you.

I realize this is a simple example of having fun with the
children, and there are also more effective and meaningful
ways of communicating your unconditional love for your
grandchildren.

Unconditional love is affection without any limitations. Each
area of expertise has a certain way of describing unconditional
love, but most will agree that it is that type of love that has
no bounds and is unchanging. Unconditional love is frequently
used to describe love between family members, comrades in
arms, and between others in highly committed relationships.
An example of this is a parent's love for her child. No matter a
test score, a life-changing decision, an argument, or a strong
belief, it doesn't affect the deep bond of love, which remains
unchanging and unconditional.

A grandfather's role is to be there for the grandchild. It is
critical for him to be supportive and understanding. He must
be more of a loving counselor than a dictator. Remember, it isn't
Grandpa's job to judge or punish a grandchild. It is his job to
love the child.

A quick note: it isn't Grandpa's job to make the child feel
guilty either, that is Grandma's job. (I know, I know; I will burn
for that one.)

Grandpa G always says, "I don't do guilt—mine or anyone's.
There is no point in it. What is done is done; move on. It only
brings pain and suffering. If Grandma wants to work with guilt,
let her, but it isn't for Grandpa."

Grandpa G was telling me a story about when one of his young teen grandsons decided to throw the computer off the roof.

> I had just arrived at my son's house, and I noticed the heavy tension in the home.
>
> So I asked my son, "What happened?"
>
> My son told me that my young grandson had decided to make a movie with his friends, showing a variety of items falling to the ground. "So he and his friends began throwing things off the roof. One of the items was an older computer, which the family still used once in a while. Of course, when it hit the ground, it was totally destroyed, with parts and pieces everywhere."
>
> My son and his wife were very upset. The poor boy received a hefty tongue-lashing and severe punishment. The boy probably deserved the punishment.
>
> When asked by his father of my thoughts, I just said, "Young teenage boys do stupid things once in a while."
>
> Then I looked at my grandson, winked, and added, "At least nobody can say he's never crashed a computer before."
>
> At that moment, my grandson looked at me and let out the biggest smile. Because he knew I didn't condemn him for making a bad decision. He understood I didn't agree with his actions, but I still saw the humor and still loved him. He knew, "Grandpa G understands me."

Love is blind. It doesn't matter what those close to you do. Nobody is perfect. Unfortunately, we sometimes make our love conditional, even when we aren't aware of it. Here is what another grandfather shared with me.

> I used to always have little projects for my grandkids to do whenever they would come over. I felt a child should be kept busy working. If they did it right, I would reward them with some sort of treat. What I didn't realize, they didn't like doing those projects. They felt the only time I

> was nice to them and showing them my love came after
> they did a good job on the project. As the grandchildren
> got older, they quit coming by as often, then hardly at all.

Because I didn't know the grandfather or his method of how he worked with his grandchildren, I can't say it is incorrect to have projects to do for grandchildren. Quite the opposite; children want to help on a project, to be a part of an accomplishment. The secret is how it is presented and how they are rewarded for being part of the project.

One grandfather was telling me about their family mountain cabin. The grandfather, along with his wife, had bought some land in the mountains with the idea of building a cabin—making it available for all the children and grandchildren. It was to be a family legacy for generations. The grandfather thought it would be good to build it with labor provided by all of the children, so it would be a work of pride for all who participated. Each would have the bragging rights to say "I helped to build the cabin!"

Everyone did pitch in, and the cabin was completed. All the children and grandchildren took great pride in knowing they were a part of the project. The grandpa said even one of his five-year-old grandchildren was telling his friend how he painted the inside of the cabin. Chuckling, the grandpa said he had to repaint the good-intention work of the five-year-old. But forever, the cabin will be the family's home in the mountains, and each will feel they were a part of its creation.

A second grandfather also understood the importance of family and how each member played an important role in its structure. Even when there are imperfections, all members need to be accepted and feel their contribution is wanted and appreciated unconditionally.

Unconditional love has been the subject of several in-depth studies, surveys, and books written about the topic. Some college courses spend many hours debating this issue. Many religions center their existence on unconditional love. Religious sermons can go on for weeks about it.

When I was at Phoenix College, a professor (Human Relations class, 1971) asked us students whether the love we had received from our parents had depended on degrees of behavior, such as how well we had succeeded in school, practiced hard for sports, been considerate toward others, or suppressed emotions like anger and fear. Unfortunately, many of us responded *yes!* It turned out that children who received this *conditional* approval were indeed somewhat more likely to act as the parent wanted just to gain higher parental approval.

But compliance came at a steep price. First, these children tended to resent and dislike their parents and grandparents. Second, they were apt to say that the manner in which they acted was often due more to a "strong internal pressure" than to "a real sense of choice." Moreover, their happiness after succeeding at something was usually short-lived, and they often felt guilty or ashamed.

After talking to mothers of grown children, it was discovered that conditional parenting often proved very damaging. Those mothers who, as children, sensed that they were loved only when they lived up to their parents' expectations now felt less worthy as adults, especially if they would make decisions they felt contradicted their parents' beliefs. Yet despite the negative effects, these mothers were more likely to use conditional affection with their own children, thus continuing the pattern.

Questions were asked of some successful, high-achieving ninth-graders at a high school in Colorado (Heritage High School, 1997) if their decisions and efforts were heavily weighted toward receiving desirable approval from parents (and grandparents). They responded that it made all the difference in the world. Their performance soared above the other ninth-graders, who had parents and grandparents who were not as involved. Acceptance from adult family members was crucial to these children, causing them to perform at a much higher level than children whose parents and grandparents were less engaged with the results.

The outcome found that both positive and negative conditional parenting were harmful, but in slightly different ways. The positive kind sometimes succeeded in getting children to work harder on academic tasks, but at the cost of unhealthy feelings of "internal compulsion." Negative conditional parenting didn't even work in the short run; it just increased the teenagers' negative feelings about their parents and grandparents.

A grandfather told me about his granddaughter:

> My granddaughter grew up in a home where her mother was always controlling her eating habits. If she ate unhealthy items, her mother would punish her by withholding affection and prevent her from seeing her friends. The daughter learned that by only eating what was approved by her mother, she could eliminate contention and punishment. However, resentment developed in the young girl toward her mother. This resentment especially appeared when she was with other friends who could have candy, pizza, and cake, while she was not permitted to partake.
>
> As she got older and away from her mother, she pushed backed. In college, she started to gain weight. After her first child, she was extremely obese. Her relationship with her mother had become sore and contentious. Even though her mother had good intentions, her method turned out to have the opposite result and created a damaged relationship. Plus, her daughter had become unhealthy.

When your love is conditional, this is the message you are sending: "I have done so much for you, so now you should do this for me." Or "I need your attention, your sympathy, your consent, your time, your presence, your love." Or "I want you to live your life according to my beliefs and ideas"; "I need you to need me—and to perform for me exactly the way I have in mind." And "if you don't do that, I will fall ill or become very unhappy." It is an attempt to control another person, which can only result in resentment.

Conditional love is an easy trap to fall into. We see and use it all the time: "If you act a certain way, then I will love you; if not, then I will withhold my love from you until you conform to my wishes." This is a very selfish love. It centers on what *you* want, not what others want or need. As a grandfather, you can't afford this kind of love in your life. Your grandchildren are counting on you *to love them no matter what they do or say.*

Every day you are tested by your grandchildren without you even knowing it. Sadly, we don't often pass the test. Usually, it comes in some form of questions, such as

- *Grandpa, what happens if I don't graduate from school?*
- *What if I fail my test you helped me study for?*
- *What if my parents get a divorce?*
- *What happens if we have to move away?*
- *If I don't do as good as my brother in school, will you still love me?*
- *Grandpa, I was thinking of getting a tattoo; what do you think?*

Despite our efforts or our desperate attempts to always do the right thing, we often fall short. When asked *what-if* questions, we seem to jump in and immediately respond with an overreaction, causing much potential trauma in the minds of our grandchildren. One grandpa shared this experience with me:

> After spending hours of practice with my grandson, working on his driver's license exam—both with the written portion and behind the wheel—my grandson was still very nervous. He asked me, "Grandpa, what if I don't pass the exam?"
>
> I immediately responded, "What do you mean, not pass the test? We have worked for hours going over every detail of the exam. You will pass the test! I didn't spend this much time with you for you to fail."

In this case, it was the grandfather who failed the test. The grandchild wasn't asking what if he failed the exam, but would Grandpa still love him if he didn't pass.

This is how wise Grandpa G handles the question:

"Grandpa, what if I don't pass the driver's license exam?" asked the grandson.

Pausing for a minute to evaluate the what-if question, Grandpa G responded, "Well . . . nothing. You won't be able to drive, and we will have to try to take it another time. I know how hard we worked on this test, but it won't change anything—I still love you, whether you pass or not. Now, let me ask you a question. If your dad lost his job, and you had to move, would it change how you felt about him? Or if your mom quit washing your clothes, would you stop loving her?"

"Well, I may not like it, but, of course, it wouldn't change how I feel about them," the child said.

"It is the same with me and how I feel about you. You see, in this family, love isn't decided by what you do or say, but on who you are to us. You are and always will be loved; nothing you can do will change that feeling we have for you."

With Grandpa G, there is always a safety net; the grandchild knows he will always be a part of the family structure, no matter what he does—and it isn't based upon his performance or choices. There is feeling of well-being, of *I am okay*. This emits an inner strength the child can rely on, allowing him to try new things without fear of failure.

But with the previous grandfather, there was no net to land on if he failed. He must perform at expected levels in order to have the assurance that he will receive the love he seeks. In this world, there always exists a deep fear that love could disappear, which results in the internal thoughts of *I can't take a chance*. Unfortunately, this can mean many lost opportunities of growth and experiences, out of fear. How sad for the young mind. This could create patterns . . . carried on throughout his life.

Some of the best advice I got from Grandpa G was, "Just love them for who they are, not for who you want them to be."

Every child comes to us with different traits unique to them. Like snowflakes, none are the same. You have to figure out their strengths versus their weaknesses, their likes and dislikes, moods, and personalities. Not that it's easy. As one parent said, "If only I had a manual with each child, life would be so much easier. They just wear me out."

Loving a grandchild unconditionally isn't always easy. There will be conflicts. Your personality may clash with theirs. Don't panic; this is normal.

As one grandfather said, "I just can't seem to get close to this grandchild. But her grandmother connects so easily with her. The child reminds me of her mother (my daughter)."

I asked, "What kind relationship did you have with your daughter, the child's mother?"

He responded, "We fought all the time."

"Why do you think that is?"

"I guess because she is just like me."

Many times, folks that have similar personalities will clash. Think of it as if it were two magnets with positive and negative poles. If you try to put the similar pole together they push away from each other, but if you put the two opposite poles together, they are attracted to each other and bond together.

There is a common belief that it is the same with people who have different personalities. If one is a talker, the other is a listener. If one is more outgoing, the other is shy. One is emotional, the other more logical. Some are very private with their feelings and thoughts, while others are very public. It is true that opposites do attract to each other. I am not saying they differ in all things, because they do have to have common interests to be together. But similar personalities often conflict.

Conflict is not necessarily a bad thing. Conflict can stimulate growth. By pushing back, we can grow stronger from it. We can develop from it, continuing to fine-tune ourselves. It can give us internal strength to move to greater accomplishments. It forces us to expand beyond our standards. It can take us out of our comfort zones. It will make us take a different look at the world and its possibilities. If children didn't have conflicting personalities with at least one parent, *they would never move out of the house.*

A typical Grandpa G saying:

> *It is like flying a kite; in order to soar to the highest heights, you have to fly against the strongest wind, not with it.*

Imagine if everyone were the same. How boring would that be? Life would be like eating food without any spices, tasteless and dull. As a grandfather you must find the things you have in common with your grandchildren. Look at their interests, not just yours. Be involved in what they like and enjoy. *Remember, you are the supporting cast member, not the main attraction.*

While unconditional love freely flows inside out, conditional love sets its terms and is directed inward. *Unconditional love is caring about the happiness of another person without any thought for what we might get for ourselves.* Unconditional love has the power to heal all wounds, bind people together, and create relationships quite beyond our present capacity to imagine. *Unconditional* means to love without regard to others' disposition toward us.

One final note: children don't need everyone to love them unconditionally. It won't come from their work, school, or even friends. But for their well-being, they do need at least one person to love them unconditionally. Grandpa, that should be you.

Chapter 7

Establishing Self-Esteem

If you think you can, you can. And if you think you can't, you're right.

—Henry Ford

What is Self-Esteem?

From *Wikipedia:*

> Self-esteem is a term in psychology to reflect a person's overall evaluation or appraisal of his or her own worth. Self-esteem encompasses beliefs (for example, "I am competent," "I am worthy") and emotions, such as triumph, despair, pride, and shame.[3] Smith and Mackie define it by saying, "The self-concept is what we think about the self; self-esteem, the positive or negative evaluation of the self, is how we feel about it."[4] Self-esteem is also known as the evaluative dimension of the self that includes feelings of worthiness, pride,

---

3   Wikipedia footnote: Hewitt, John P. (2009). *Oxford Handbook of Positive Psychology.* Oxford University Press, pp. 217–224.

4   Wikipedia footnote: Smith, E. R.; Mackie, D. M. (2007). *Social Psychology* (Third ed.). Hove: Psychology Press, p. 107.

and discouragement.[5] One's self-esteem is also closely associated with self-consciousness.

Every person has a mental picture of who he or she is, how he or she looks, what he or she is good at, and what consists of his or her weaknesses. This concept or picture is not developed overnight, but over time, from the infant stages to old age. Our self-image is constantly changing, day by day, year by year, creating new mental pictures of oneself through interaction with those around us and normal experiences throughout life. The mental picture we see affects our self-esteem.

Therefore, how we feel loved and how we see our abilities can establish our understanding of ourselves and of those who contribute to our self-esteem. Low self-esteem can be created by a child who feels loved but doesn't feel good about his abilities. Low self-esteem can also occur in a child who is confident in her abilities but doesn't feel loved. A good balance has to be developed for a positive, healthy self-esteem to be maintained.

Self-esteem patterns start very early in one's life. Children come into this world like a blank canvas of art, with no preconceived ideas of who they are, totally innocent of all knowledge. The process of creating self-esteem will begin developing from the moment of birth, established by how the child is held and nurtured. There will be many *artists* (parents, grandparents, siblings, friends, teachers, and family) contributing to that self-esteem canvas, creating an image of how each child sees him or herself. Successfully creating a positive self-image takes persistence, and deserves major effort in the child's young life. Once we reach adulthood, it's harder to make changes in how we see and define ourselves.

That's why it's recommended to think about developing and promoting self-esteem during childhood. As children try, fail, try again, fail again, and then finally succeed, they develop ideas about their own capabilities. To help them through the

---

5   Wikipedia footnote: Newman, Barbara M.; Newman, Philip R. (1975). *Development Through Life: A Psychosocial Approach*. Homewood, IL: Dorsey.

process, their involvement with those around them is key to their successful development. This is where grandparents— *especially Grandpa*—can help the children create healthy and correct self-perceptions.

Grandpa G gave me this example:

> My five-year-old grandson decided he wanted jam on his sandwich. He asked if I could get it for him. I told him it was in the refrigerator door and to try to get it for himself. I realized I could have gotten it for him, but I wanted to see what he would do. The jam was a heavy, fifty-ounce jar on the top, inside-door shelf. Since his head only came to the middle of the refrigerator, I knew he couldn't reach the jar.
>
> Feeling up to the challenge, the boy went and got a chair and dragged it to the refrigerator door. After standing on the chair, he realized he still couldn't reach high enough to get the leverage to lift the heavy jar out of the tray. He got back down, moved the chair closer; then he retried. This time, he was able to lift the jar, but he couldn't get a good grip to lift it above the shelf rim. It was too heavy, and so he dropped it back into the slot.
>
> At that moment, I decided to go help him; then a thought came to me to wait and see what he did. Looking at it for a moment, he moved another jar next to the jam and put it on a different shelf in the refrigerator. Then having enough room to get a better grip on the jar of jam, he carefully lifted it out. Knowing he didn't have a great grip, he eased it onto a lower shelf of the door. Once the jam was safely secured on the shelf, he pushed the chair a bit away from the door. Then he got back on it to get hold of the jar. Then he put the jar on the chair while he got down. After that, he proceeded to pick up the jar and go and place it on the countertop. Returning to the refrigerator, he replaced the other jar back on the top shelf! Having completed that, he moved the chair away and closed the door. With a big smile on his face, he gave me a thumbs-up.

I told him how smart he was to figure out the jam's retrieval. When he finished with the jam, he did everything in reverse order.

If I left it there, saying nothing more about the task, all would be fine, but I had a different plan. I waited until his parents walked into the room—while he was still there. I then proceeded to tell them, in front of him, how clever and smart he was to figure it out by himself and how proud I was of him. His little eyes and face were just beaming. He felt good about what he did and that I was proud of him. It may have been a simple task for me, but it was a major accomplishment for him. That day, his self-esteem took a very positive jolt.

Grandparents and caregivers can promote healthy self-esteem by showing encouragement and recognition in many areas of a child's young life. It isn't necessary to focus in any one area, for example math or grades, but all activities that involve the child.

For a child to have a hearty self-esteem, it isn't about promoting or bragging about accomplishments, it is more about understanding the child's strengths and weaknesses. Self-esteem is not all about how much children feel valued, loved, accepted, and thought well of by others. It is more about how much they value, love, and accept themselves.

Children with healthy self-esteem are able to feel good about themselves, while appreciating their own worth, taking pride in their abilities, skills, and accomplishments. Children with low self-esteem may feel as if no one will like them or accept them as they are or that they can't do well in anything. This is especially true with children through their developing years, when their abilities are in their nascent stages.

Some children have been blessed with abilities to be good at many things. This can create high self-esteem regarding their accomplishments. They will often compare their successes against other children. When they perform at a higher level, it can cause a *superior* attitude not just healthy self-esteem. Even though one's self-worth is important, it must be contained within certain boundaries. All children, just like adults, have things they're good at and things that are difficult for them. If challenges become too easy for some children, then it may be necessary to find more challenging tasks.

One young woman was telling me about her brother. He was a very bright young man. He had many talents. Academics were extremely easy for him. His physical abilities were also very advanced. In every sport, he succeeded. His verbal skills were unmatched. Even his looks helped promote him. He had little or no challenges.

Because of these talents, he started becoming arrogant toward his siblings, his parents, and friends. Fights were frequent and hurtful. She continued:

> One day my grandfather, after noticing the conflict, made a suggestion to my parents. He knew of his grandson's easy lifestyle and told my parents to find something that would require more effort from him. He recommended a skill that would be hard for him to accomplish—for instance, a musical instrument.
>
> So my parents bought my brother a violin. He hated it. He couldn't breeze through the practice like he was able to in other avenues of his life. It was unseemly difficult for him. He had to practice every day. Over a long time, he was finally able to master the instrument. He was never great at it, but it forced him to overcome a major challenge in his young life. Grandpa's suggestion changed his life.
>
> As we have gotten older, he has become very successful. Every time I visit his office, I see the violin leaning against the wall. I asked him why he leaves it out. He told me whenever he starts to feel overconfident or comes across a difficult situation, he will start to play the violin to remind him of weaknesses and strengths. He says it brings him back to reality. It allows him to refocus on problems and tasks to bring him to the basics.

All individuals experience problems with self-esteem at certain times in their lives. This is particularly true in the teenage years, when young people are figuring out who they are and where they fit in the world. The good news is that, because everyone's self-image changes over time, self-esteem is not fixed for life. It is never too late to help someone to improve it. If you can help a child see him or herself in a realistic, positive, truthful way, it will encourage a better understanding of strengths and weaknesses and still have great self-esteem.

How a child sees himself can influence how he lives his life. Children who feel that they're likable and lovable have better relationships. They're more likely to ask for help and support from friends and family when they need it. Children who believe they can accomplish goals and solve problems are more likely to do well in school. Having healthy self-esteem allows a child to accept himself and live a better life.

Courage comes from having strong self-esteem. It empowers a child to believe in himself and try new things. It allows him to respect himself, even when he makes mistakes. If a child shows respect for himself, adults and other kids usually respect him too.

Healthy self-esteem is like a child's armor against the challenges of the world. Children who know their strengths and weaknesses and feel good about themselves seem to have an easier time handling conflicts and resisting negative pressures. They tend to smile, be happier, and enjoy life. These children see things with less stress, are realistic, and generally optimistic.

In contrast, children with low self-esteem can find challenges to be sources of major anxiety and frustration. They have a harder time facing problems and finding solutions to them. Self-critical thoughts such as *I'm worthless* or *I can't do anything right,* may cause them to become passive, withdrawn, or depressed. The thought *I can't* is too often the response when a new challenge arises.

Positive self-esteem puts children in a positive mind-set, so they may make good choices concerning their own health— both mental and physical. Having positive self-value gives a person the power to say no when confronted with a group of friends who are doing something inappropriate, wrong, or dangerous. Strong self-worth helps a child make wise and responsible decisions on her own. It allows children to have their own value systems concerning feelings, health, beliefs, spirituality, and body. Every part of them is valued, which should be and will be protected by them.

Chapter 8

Building Self-Image

Self-image can get children where they want to go, and getting there is a daily process. It's so much easier when they feel good about themselves, their abilities, and talents.

—Grandpa G

When babies are born, they don't have any opinion of themselves in a good or bad way. They don't think *I'm wonderful!* when they let out a smile or worry *oh no, this outfit makes me look fat!* Instead, people around the baby helps him or her develop self-worth. How? Through encouragement, often clapping when the baby learns to crawl, walk, or talk. They often offer praises, "Great job. Good for you!" Or, they might just smile and look proud. When people take good care of a baby, that alone can help the child feel loved and valuable.

As children get older, they can have a bigger role in developing their own self-worth. Working hard to finish a school project or assignment, getting a better grade on a math test, or trying out for a new sport are all things children can do to receive self-worth for trying. Some children are not very athletic, but they might be good readers, or they might be good in drama or art; others may know how to do magic tricks. Still others might be good at making friends or providing a service to people. All of these accomplishments help children feel good about themselves.

A child's family and other people in his or her life—like coaches, teachers, friends, spiritual leaders, and classmates—can have a major impact in boosting self-worth. They can help a child figure out how to do things or notice his or her good qualities. They can believe in the child and inspire him or her to try again when something doesn't go right the first time. It's all part of children's learning to see themselves in positive ways, to feel proud of what they've done, and to be confident that there's a lot more they can do. Their worth is in their contribution to a group. When they feel they are valued and needed, it sends a message to oneself: *I am important and I matter.*

In order for a child to overcome self-worth problems and develop a healthy self-image, we first have to know what might cause those problems in the first place. The two biggest factors which come into play are how others see or treat them and how they see and treat themselves.

A few years ago, a teacher became very famous from her method of teaching. It changed the attitude of many and challenged the established standards in the teaching world. Marva Collins started her own school after being dissatisfied with the school district's lack of education among children in inner-city schools. She started with children who often had the lowest grade scores and worst backgrounds. Many were not wanted in the regular schools because of behavior and low-skill performance. Ms. Collins was able to overcome the obstacles. Her students achieved high levels in test scores, and behavioral problems disappeared. She overcame the obstacles through showing love for each child, being positive, and not being willing to give up on the students.

She taught never to write anything negative about a child; test scores showed only positive statements. She never used words like *that's wrong* or showed failing grades, for example.

When a child would take a test, Ms. Collins would evaluate it with notes like this: "Do you know out of ten questions, you got three correct? You are so smart and wonderful."

Every comment was done with praise. If Tommy went to the blackboard and tried to spell a word, such as *tree*, and misspelled it *trye*, the response would be, "Tommy, you know you got three of the letters correct; you are such an intelligent child. The correct way to spell is t-r-e-e. I know if you practice tonight, when you come back tomorrow, you will remember how to spell *tree.*"

At the beginning of each school year, Marva Collins would have the official report cards already filled out for each child. They were all As and Os (O for outstanding). She would tell each child, "This is your true grade, and the only way you can change it is if you don't come to class and listen to the lessons."

Her teaching method was all done by praise, never any negative comparisons with work from other students or papers marked red with how many questions were missed. Children who came out of her classes had a solid self-worth and self-image of themselves. They went on to have very successful lives, ready to face any challenges in their paths.

Parents, grandparents, teachers, religious leaders, and other authority figures influence the ideas children are developing about themselves—particularly, little children. If those in authority spend more time criticizing than praising a child, it can be harder for a child to develop good self-value. When they become teens and are still forming their own values and beliefs, it can be easy to build self-image around what a grandparent, parent, coach, or almost any other person says.

Obviously, self-esteem can be damaged when someone whose acceptance is important (like a parent, grandparent, or teacher) constantly puts you down. But criticism doesn't have to come from other people. Most teens are constantly doing self-evaluations—a voice inside that seems to find fault with everything they do. Sometimes that inner voice is unintentionally modeled on a critical parent or grandparent's voice. As a grandpa, it is critical we do not add to the negative inner tapes playing in our grand-teens' heads.

Everyone plays tapes in their mind of the influences from their childhoods, positive or negative. Over time, listening to a negative inner voice can harm a person's self-esteem just as much as if the criticism were coming from another person. Some people get so used to their inner mental voice being mean that they don't even notice when they're putting themselves down.

Unrealistic expectations can also affect someone's self-worth. People have an image of who they want to be (or who they think they should be). Everyone's image of the ideal person is different. For example, some people admire athletic skills, and others admire music or academic abilities. Still others model their moral beliefs from religious ideals of proper behavior.

How an individual is treated often determines his or her outcome in life. If those close to them see the child as dumb, ugly, or untalented then the child will accept that model for himself. It becomes real to him. On the opposite side, if a child is made to feel he or she is special, talented, needed, and beautiful, they will become more so in their actions and performances.

One individual was telling me of his experience with his grandfather. He began,

> I was a middle child who often got lost in recognition. My brother was outstanding in all he did, receiving constant praise from my father and mother. My younger sister was the fair child—smart, beautiful, and very talented. Me, I was athletically challenged, an average student with no particular skills. When we would meet new people, my parents would sing praises about my brother and sister. I was always the afterthought, the unnoticed child. My opinions were never taken seriously. My ideas were always rejected in favor of my siblings. In my parents' home, I was like furniture—taking up space but not noticed. My parents even left me two times on trips, driving away for several miles before they realized I wasn't in the car. I once heard my dad tell someone he didn't expect me to amount to much when I grew up.
>
> Then one spring, everything changed when we went to visit Grandpa Dulley at his dairy farm. I was only

eleven years old. All of us got to help in the chores for the farm. The chores included things like loading hay, putting hay into the troughs to feed the cows, herding the cows to the milk shed, cleaning them off before putting on the milking machines, and various other activities.

That year, Grandpa called me over and told me he had a special job just for me. At a dairy farm, one item that is produced in abundance is manure. It is everywhere. Grandpa told me he wanted me to drive the tractor and grade all of the manure into a pile so he could sell it.

I told Grandpa I was only eleven; I didn't know how to drive a tractor. Grandpa was not a man who you could easily change his mind. He just said, "I will show you." Besides, he said he knew I was the best man for the job. For the next three hours, he patiently showed me everything: the important things—like how to drive using the gears, the brakes, to work the back grader and the front shovel scoop. He taught me how to keep my lines straight, move into tight places, and plan ahead. During the following several days I drove that tractor, gathering all the manure into one big pile. I won't say that first time it was a great job, but it made me feel good about myself and what I could do.

My siblings and my cousins were so jealous of me. When one would ask Grandpa if he or she could drive the tractor, he would just say, "Nope, that job is his," pointing to me, "and nobody could do it better." I was on cloud nine, so happy. Even when my dad asked Grandpa if I wasn't too young to have such a responsibility of handling the expensive machinery, Grandpa just responded, "It isn't his age, it's his ability to do the job," and that I was the best one of all the grandchildren. Thanks to Grandpa, all of a sudden I mattered, I was important, I could do great work. My confidence level shot through the roof.

For several years, I would go to Grandpa's house every chance I got to work with the tractor. I became an expert with machinery. At age eighteen, I earned a job with a big construction company, being a finish-grader for special projects. Eventually, I started my own very successful company. I am now retired, very financially stable, while my brother and sister are still working.

Grandpa saw something in me that my parents didn't see. He gave me a chance to become something, which wasn't available to me in my own home, for they only saw me as average. But Grandpa saw me at a higher level. Grandpa was a wise man.

This story reminds me of a quote from Johann Wolfgang von Goethe, a well-known German author: "If you treat an individual as he is, he will remain as he is, but if you treat him as he ought to be, could be, and would be, then he will become what he ought to be, can be, and shall be."

Recognizing the symptoms of low self-esteem is a necessary step to understand a child's needs. Self-worth fluctuates as children grow. It's frequently changed and fine-tuned, because it is affected by a child's experiences and new perceptions. So it helps to be aware of the signs of both healthy and unhealthy self-image. As a grandparent, your influence can greatly affect the child's view of himself or herself.

Children with low self-worth may not want to try new things and may speak negatively about themselves: "I'm stupid"; "I'll never learn how to do this," or "What's the point? Nobody cares about me anyway." They might exhibit a low tolerance for frustration, giving up easily or waiting for somebody else to take over. They lean toward being overly critical of themselves and are easily disappointed. Positive reinforcement from a grandfather can counter the negative feelings demonstrated by some children.

Children with low self-image see temporary setbacks as permanent, insurmountable problems, and a sense of worst-case scenario prevails. This can place children at risk for stress and mental-health problems. Facing and solving problems may become an extreme mental task for them. A grandfather who provides a safe-listening support and a willingness to help can change the outcome.

Children with healthy self-worth tend to enjoy interacting with others more. They're comfortable in social settings and enjoy group activities. They can do well with independent pursuits. When challenges arise, they can find solutions and work with others in positive ways. They don't use words such as "I'm an idiot," "I can't do this," "this is too hard for me," or "I don't understand this." They know their strengths and weaknesses and accept them. A sense of optimism prevails. We, as grandfathers, can encourage and praise them to reinforce their successes.

Some children have positive self-esteem, but then something happens in their lives to change that. For example:

If a child moves and doesn't make friends right away at the new school, he might start to feel bad and think he is not desirable enough to be someone's good friend.

Children whose parents divorce might find that this can affect self-image. They may feel bad when a parent can't give them attention or come to their game, because they are not together any more. Many will do the blame-game, thinking if they had behaved better or kept their room cleaner, their parents would not have split up. Grandfathers have a great opportunity to step up and take some of the load or burden from parents with children who are experiencing this situation in their lives. A bond can be made that will renew the child's strength and confidence.

Some children can develop a phobia about their looks from things they have no control over, such as illnesses like asthma or cancer, birthmarks, glasses, or other physical restrictions. They can feel that they stand out from others, that they are not normal, especially if they are being made fun of by other children.

Some have learning or speaking difficulties that contribute to an atmosphere of fear and self-doubt and leave them feeling less important or unequal to other children. They can start to lose confidence in themselves. Grandfathers can help provide simple projects with positive outcomes that allow the child to achieve success.

Make your grandchildren feel special to you in your life. Talk about specific character traits, family traditions, and their heritage. Make them feel good about who they are.

Unfortunately, a child's family makeup can have an effect; for example, an overachiever in the family might be setting unrealistic goals for the rest of the children. This can create the impression of failure or a feeling of *I am not as good.* Each child needs to feel special about his own performance. Grandpa can and must find ways to brag about each child.

Be aware of potential insecurities, such as when a child's body is going through the changes of puberty; this can affect a child's self-esteem. Children's emotional and physical changes can send them and those around them into high stress and tension.

As one grandfather said, "If you aren't patient with a teenager, you will both burn in hell."

Being in tune with the children's circumstances is a necessary requirement to understanding them.

Chapter 9

Abstain from Criticism

To some, criticism is a form of flattery; to most, it is a form of jealousy, hate, and feeling superior.

—Grandpa G

One of the biggest regrets mentioned by grandpas was their use of criticism. They said they had often criticized their grandchildren without thinking, because of impatience, being tired, in the name of humor, or just because they could. After they saw the hurt feelings, the burden of regret for their harsh words was felt. Some grandfathers were just aloof, staying away from any kind of involvement, and when confronted, they would sometimes criticize.

One individual was telling me how he hated to go to Grandpa's house when he was young.

"Twice a year our family went to visit Grandpa. I hated it," he told me.

I asked why.

"Because Grandpa would just sit there, never doing anything with us. Sure, he would say hi and ask a few questions, but that was the extent of it," he explained.

"That doesn't seem bad; why did you dislike being there?" I questioned.

"It was because of the rules. We couldn't go into certain parts of the house. We weren't allowed to touch any of the things around the house. The garage was off-limits. There was no place to play. He didn't have any toys. If we did touch something, he would chew us out. He was constantly telling us that we were too loud, too active, too sticky, and too messy. Grandpa was just a grumpy old man. He criticized everything we did," he said.

"Do you think he didn't like you?" I asked.

"No, we all knew he loved us; he just didn't have any patience with us. Maybe he forgot how to be around children. I doubt he even knew how harsh he was with us," he explained.

Sometimes it can be easy for an adult to criticize. Children can be very frustrating. They don't usually listen. Kids push the envelope as far as they can. Fighting can be a normal occurrence with siblings, raising tension levels in the home. *They run, they jump, and they yell.* All children do things they know they aren't supposed to do and then look you in the eye and say they didn't do it. Kids will interrupt an adult who is involved in an important activity or conversation to ask a trivial question. Little ones spill drinks, drop food, and touch things with sticky hands. They draw on walls, don't put things away, and splash water everywhere in bathrooms, kitchens, family rooms, and hallways. When the news the grandchildren are coming to visit arrives, it will send grandparents into a frenzy trying to childproof the house before they get there.

No grandchild is perfect. Sometimes grandpas forget that. To be overly critical is not acceptable. Often we see things from a higher level of experience—from an adult's rather than a child's point of view. What is old hat to us can be a world of wonder to a little child.

One grandpa was telling me how he had forgotten the wonder of the world from a child's point of view. So he decided to try looking at the world from a lower level . . . literally.

He told me, "I spent the day on my hands and knees with my granddaughter, looking at things. One of the best things we shared together was staring through the glass oven door at the pizza cooking in the oven. It was fun watching the melting cheese and bubbling pizza while it cooked. It was a gift that day to see excitement in a world I had lost through my changing into adulthood. Through her eyes, I had a chance to relive my own childhood. Now, most people would say *how boring.* But because I was with my granddaughter, at her level, we bonded. I learned a lot that day. Sometimes in our adult world, we miss the simple joys of life, long lost from childhood."

Often we will have a superior attitude, thinking children should act like adults, and then criticize them for not doing so. Yet, we have forgotten what it was like being a child. Sometimes we just need to take a moment, step back from the situation, and reflect on the idea: they are children without our knowledge or experience. Many times, we just need to be patient and give them a break.

As Grandpa G says, "Talk to them as you would have someone talk to you . . . if *you* made a mistake."

There is an old saying, which applies: "There are two ways to build the highest building. One is to tear down all the buildings around yours, leaving yours as the tallest building, higher than the rest. The second is to build a taller building."

Our goal is to build them up by bringing the grandchildren to a higher level, not knocking them down.

I have wondered why individuals criticize others, especially children. Here are some explanations for the behavior. If you see yourself doing this, think about it.

1. *I am just being real.* Many grandfathers think that they are just being realistic. They want to help and whip the children into shape, toughen them up so they can face the world. Could they say so in a kinder fashion? They agree that they could do it in a nicer fashion, but they strongly believe that being nice may not drive home the point.

2. *This is the way I am; deal with it.* With some grandpas, this is their style, and that is who they are—it's hard for them to change their ways now. Many grandfathers don't seem to have a problem with their abrasive style, and some of them were convinced they were working on changing the child for the better.

3. *Surprised to hear it!* Some of the grandfathers I talked to were surprised that they came across as "extremely critical." They thought that they were just having a heart-to-heart conversation.

4. *I really care.* Some grandpas think that their caring cannot possibly come across as "being critical." If they didn't care, they reported, they would have not participated in the discussion in the first place. Once they start participating, all stops were removed.

5. *I am a passionate person.* Some grandfathers thought that they were so passionate on a topic, if they went too far, it was because they got carried away, but it was good for the children to see their passion.

6. *I am just being honest.* These grandpas believe honesty is the best policy and that the focus has to be on the message and not about the way the message is delivered. It is unfair to be penalized for honesty, they feel.

7. *I am only teasing them.* In the disguise of humor, some grandfathers will say very hurtful and insensitive words. They will often criticize or ridicule, thinking it is funny. But what may be funny to an adult can rock a little one's world, creating harsh feelings of self-doubt and extreme embarrassment. These are the kinds of feelings that can leave deep emotional scars for a long time.

8. *Criticizing others makes it about me, not them.* Sometimes, grandfathers sadly take a superior attitude when dealing with grandchildren. You hear comments like, "Don't argue with me; I'm the grandfather," or "When you get to be my age, then you can have an opinion." Having more knowledge and experience doesn't give a person the right to judge, criticize, or ridicule, especially as children are going through the learning process. Abusing authority only promotes anger and resentment.

Children of all ages make mistakes. Criticize as you would be criticized.

> *Before you go and criticize the younger generation, just remember who raised them.*
> —Unknown

Chapter 10

How Boys and Girls are Different

Grandpa, why does Tarah do things different from me?
She doesn't think like I do.

—Grandchild

To understand children, it needs to be done at a basic level—by starting with the differences between boys and girls. Boys and girls have different thought patterns, which carry on into adulthood. If one can grasp the diverse nature of how boys and girls view the world around them, then a grandfather will be able to better relate to their needs and development.

Males have different cell and body makeup than females. This means, they are not the same at a basic physical structure down to the gene level. This affects their thought processes, physical requirements, and developmental progression. It allows both to function better in their designed roles as parents and opposite partners. By looking at their own environment through separate viewpoints, the results can be dramatic. Yet at the same time, they can complement each other, causing a higher level of accomplishment. This is why males and females need each other to perform parenting and other tasks for the best success.

Even as children, one will notice how males and females go about performing and addressing challenges or assignments given to them in different ways. Males will say words like "I think" while females will use words like "I feel." Boys will relate to things with their head, while girls will relate to things with their heart. Males lean to function more by using the left side of the brain versus females doing activities using the right side of the brain. In other words, males work with logic compared to females embracing emotion. Don't misunderstand, many females work with logic and many males work with emotion.

The significance of this directly affects their self-worth and self-image. Boys usually develop their viewed value through accomplishments, while girls will often gather their self-value from being accepted and loved. Girls need to feel good about who they are, while boys need to feel good about what they have done.

As a grandparent, if one knows the difference between the gender tendencies of the grandchildren, it becomes valuable in coping and meeting their needs.

There was an experiment done with children at play in my high school many years ago (East Phoenix High School, Family Living class) to see how they addressed different activities and objects. One of the tests was done by putting different items in a room with boys and girls. One item was a round, metallic object painted in a beautiful design. When a girl saw it, she picked it up, admired the colors, held it up to the light, and said, "How beautiful." The boy picked it up, checked the weight, tossing it up and down a few times, and then threw it against the wall. We found boys were drawn to hard objects in shapes of animals, cars, houses, and people, especially if they had moving parts. The girls were attracted to items that were soft and colorful. Dolls and household products also caught their attention.

The class continued to observe how the children played. The boys would find things to hit, throw, bounce, and jump on. The girls would find things to touch, draw, paint, play princess, have tea parties, and create stories. Girls would be more social, seeking out others to play with, while boys often played happily alone. Girls did more verbal activities, but boys did more physical. When groups of boys played together, they would play physical, competitive games together. Girl groups would do more verbal activities, games, make-believe, and drama. When the boys and girls groups were put together, the games girls liked the best were games such as hide-and-seek, tag, word games, dramas, and board games. Games most liked by the boys were sports-related—throwing, catching, shooting, physically challenging and competitive games.

Our study also revealed older children had the tendency to control the activities and games. Younger ones would follow, trying to fit in with the older children. Patterns of play would transfer down to each younger age group. For instance, a bossy attitude of the oldest children would be repeated by younger children when they would play with children younger still.

The biggest results of the experiment determined that girls preferred individual interactions versus boys preferring competitive, individual success. The motivation of girls who did "boys' sports" was in order to be accepted. The motivation of boys doing "girls' activities" was because they felt they had to or were manipulated into it, even if they enjoyed the activity.

Knowing what children enjoy makes it easier to understand and address their needs. Being able to recognize the differences between girls and boys will help you be a better support in their lives. Again, I stress this observation is not absolute. Behavior can and will be shaped depending on their upbringing and environment. This is based on most boys and girls. But still boys and girls are different. They don't think the same or relate the same. They don't respond the same. Girls are stimulated by words, while boys are stimulated by sight (physical). Boys gain self-esteem by accomplishments, girls by love and relations.

In one interview, this is what a young woman relayed to me:

> "My grandfather came to all my games."
>
> I asked, "Why do you think he came?"
>
> "Because he wanted to see me play . . . and to support me," she said.

Another survey done by a young man had a slightly different view.

"Grandpa would come to our games," he said.
Again I asked, "Why do you think he came to the games?"
"He liked the sport, wanted to see how we played, and to watch us win," he responded.

This was their first response. It doesn't mean that either grandfather didn't love the child or go to enjoy the game, because each child needs to see both from a grandpa. It just reflects their first thought how they saw the reason for their grandpa attending.

The two individuals fondly remembered their grandfathers coming to the games, but for two different reasons. She believed he came because of his care for her and the relationship, while the boy believed his grandpa came to see what he did and how he performed. Again proving girls visualize relationships and boys see accomplishments.

There is however one way both of the sexes are the same. This is in becoming of age. When children become teenagers, they begin the first stages of adulthood. They begin to see themselves as more independent and to have their own opinions. Their understanding and thinking can be on a higher plane. If you look back to a few hundred years ago when the pioneers and early settlers of the country got married, it was often in the middle or even early teen years. The average age of death was in the thirties. By their twenties, they were middle-aged. Many of our ancestors who married would be considered children in our current day. They were forced to be adults at a young age. Yet, they met the challenges with good decisions and strong character.

Granted, they were not fully mature or experienced in life situations, but they were quick to form ideas, opinions, make adult decisions, and have desires of an adult.

Today, if you have a teenager in the house, you have an adult—this is especially true of girls. They have opinions, desires, and ideas like an adult. Even though they may still be immature, they have the base of an adult. This can cause conflict between mothers and daughters—two adult females in one home. Grandpa, as a father and grandfather, it is important to recognize this when talking to your children. Interacting with a teenager is much different from dealing with a younger child. Their thoughts are at a higher level and deserve to be recognized as valuable input.

One individual told the following story about her relationship with her grandfather when she was a teenager.

> When I was a teenager, I was constantly fighting with my mom. She never understood me. I had to deal with unfair restrictions and outdated beliefs. If I went to my dad, he would just take mom's side, even if he knew I was right. She treated me like I was a small child, not letting me make my own decisions. I hated it there. I was thinking about running away.
>
> Then Grandpa moved close to us. It changed everything. He was my refuge against the storm. I would go over to his house whenever conflict arose. He would just listen, not judging, just hearing my side of the story. He treated me with respect, as an adult. Often by explaining the problem, I would find solutions without the emotions associated at my home.
>
> He never told me I was wrong or making mistakes. He would only ask questions to get everything out in the open. Sometimes, he would tell a joke or make me laugh to ease the tension. Because of this, I was able to figure out things for myself. If I needed advice, he would give it; if not, he didn't. Grandpa saved me through those teenage years.

Chapter 11

The Power of a Compliment

*A compliment is sunshine to your soul. I can live two
weeks on a good compliment.*

—Mark Twain

One of the most effective ways to help children build self-
esteem is through praise and compliments.

There isn't anybody who doesn't like compliments; it doesn't
matter who you are. We all enjoy it when someone notices us
and makes a positive statement to us or about us. We all like to
be noticed for our good qualities, no matter what they might be.
When we compliment someone, we are expressing admiration,
affection, or respect—perhaps all three—for something about
that person.

If you want to develop a good relationship with someone or
bond with them, the best way to start is giving them a sincere
compliment. When we compliment someone, we are sending
them a message *about them,* something positive we see in them.
Positive observations by others lifts us up, and this can have a
bonding effect.

Each of us knows how good it makes us feel when someone
compliments us. We have experienced the sensation of pleasure
that comes from a compliment given by others. But all too
often we fail to recognize how good someone might feel to get

a compliment from us, even with the knowledge of how good compliments make us feel.

Responses to compliments will be bonding in nature, nearly every time. You will hear it, see it, and feel it in those responses you receive from those you are complimenting. Most of us demonstrate a positive response when we are complimented. Our natural response is to treat kindness with kindness. Those nice responses often help open the door to further conversation with that person, and compliments, because they are an expression of kindness, can be very bonding.

Compliments draw people toward you. Compliments are like magnets of attraction, especially when said at the right time. Compliments are positive connections with another person. When you compliment someone you are saying, "I like you," and if you are not fond of the person, it conveys a message of I accept you or accept what you have done.

Giving a genuine compliment allows you to come out of yourself. This is because it requires you to be observant of those around you. When you are observant of those around you, it becomes much easier to find sincere praises about them. And the more often you are able to make those compliments, the more opportunities you have of creating a bond with your grandchildren and other family members.

Compliments can affect everyone involved, including you, in a positive way. For example, we all have things going on in our lives that make things look not as bright as we might like. A compliment from another person can help us put things into a more appealing picture, depending on the consequences of the compliment. Now, turn that scenario around: if your compliment helps a person to see things differently, more acceptably or in a more positive light, it makes them more open and happier, and you have just started creating a bond. You will have helped them see that good things still exist, even if things look bleak to them right then.

Okay, if the truth be known, I believe most men don't understand how nor do a good job of giving compliments.

There is a sad story about a man who never gave his wife any compliments. At her funeral, he was staring at her in the casket and talking to a friend. He said, "She was a good woman, and I almost told her so once."

Don't let this happen to you.

Grandpa G explained a little about compliments.

> When I first started giving compliments, I was awkward and shy about it. I kept wondering if I'd offend the person in some way or make people suspicious about what I wanted from them. I've since discovered that a sincere compliment is always a welcome boost to someone's day. There will be those who reject it or will even argue with you, but that's usually their problem and not mine. A compliment is like a present, if someone doesn't want your present, you'll still end up owning it. You'll also find when you start noticing good things about people, they will notice more good things about you too! And the more you do, the more pleasure you will receive in sharing compliments.

Women, for the most part, have learned how to give compliments. From childhood to adults, they are encouraged to share their positive thoughts and praises. For them, sharing a compliment is part of a nurturing instinct, passed down through mothers to daughters. Praising an individual is like water running downhill, little effort or thought goes into it. However, it is different for men.

There are a few men who have been taught how to give compliments and praises. These few can express elaborate phrases that roll off their tongues like water off a duck's back. Many of them have been schooled by older sisters and mothers. But for most of us, men as a group haven't developed these techniques by ourselves. We men haven't had the opportunity to observe other men using the art of praising on a regular basis. It isn't because we don't want to give compliments to those around us—in most cases, we just don't know how or, even worse, think about it. Men will go through phases where we will try to use complimentary words, but we are usually not consistent for long periods of time. There are exceptions of course. Some cultures place a value on verbalizing praise; unfortunately, as a whole ours does not.

The Art of Giving a Compliment

In order to make compliments come across as real and meaningful words of praise, it takes a dedicated effort not standard in most men's lives. Unfortunately, it is becoming an increasingly elusive treasure. The reality is that the art of giving meaningful compliments has become a dying one. And yet, in our hearts, most of us have a longing to give meaningful compliments that leave a lasting impression. To do this, it needs to be a matter of simplicity and intent.

We rush our words or we rehearse them, instead of allowing the compliment to organically emerge. They have to come out naturally to feel sincere. It isn't easy to do if you don't have a pattern to follow. It is sad most men didn't have a father whom they could watch to learn the art of complimenting. The days of the John Wayne-like pattern of grab-them-and-kiss-them approach (or I call it the caveman proposal to courtship) is giving way to more gentle romantic tactics. I am not saying that John Wayne's approach isn't desired, but sometimes both approaches are wanted. In terms of grandchildren, the rough, silent tough guy approach may not be as appealing as the more praising and verbally encouraging appeal.

In the surveys, it was surprising how common this characteristic of sharing or giving compliments was mentioned. When asked if a grandfather gave compliments to his grandchildren, here was a typical response: "Sure I do. I just told my grandson today that he didn't drop the ball, like he normally does."

Here were some others:

- Hey, I see you have on a red dress today.
- You already finished working on the car this afternoon.
- I like the way your hair covers your big ears.

- It took you a long time, but you did finally finish the homework.

These are not compliments; yet to some, because they make a comment about an activity or notice and mention an item in their mind, it is a compliment.

With Grandpa's G help, I put together some guidelines on creating and delivering stimulating and compassionate compliments.

Be Sincere

You can throw out a hundred compliments during a conversation, but unless you seem sincere when you say them, you're not going to get a good response from that person. Without seeming clichéd, you want to give compliments from the heart. Truly mean what you're saying to the person, especially children. They can spot a phony comment immediately. Otherwise, a person may just see you as a fake, insincere person, with the possibility of your relationship being questioned.

Meaning what you say is important for it to be a meaningful compliment. Be careful, because we often have the skill and experience when talking to children to use platitudes that seem specific enough to pacify a child. Despite your knack for false sincerity, most children can tell when your words aren't genuine. That's why you shouldn't force a compliment just because it somehow seems like the time or place to offer one.

Sincerity must be real, a genuine heartfelt emotion. To throw out a compliment because it seems like a good thing to do or circumstances lend to it, if done without real meaning, is a waste and usually not accepted. If you don't feel it, then don't say anything.

Be Specific

Detail is the lifeblood of good praising. It's also the heart of a great compliment. Hone in on a specific achievement or aspect, and focus your words on that. A vague, generalized comment that can be recycled throughout the day such as "You look good today" or "Great job" lacks real meaning, because of its cookie-cutter nature.

Specific compliments have lasting power. So do those that favor character over objects or outward appearance. They indicate that you've truly taken stock of a person and their attributes and, in turn, compressed those thoughts into a value judgment.

> Today you look fantastic; I love the ruffled look of your hair—it shows your rugged nature and outstanding personality.
>
> You did a great job today in cleaning the garage, putting all the items away. Plus, working on your own without needing help shows you are growing up fast and you can be trusted to make good decisions.

Look For The Extraordinary

In order to give a good compliment, you need to keep your focus looking for something that a person does well. Focusing on complimenting things over which the person has control, like their kindness to others, rather than things over which they have no control, like their looks, can be the most powerful. Pick something that really stands out, and don't give a generic compliment. Learn to be original in using compliments.

A grandpa was mentioning how he used to have a large fish mounted in his home on the den wall. He said he finally took it down, because every person who came into the den would comment on the fish. It would dominate their conversations to the point he grew tired of discussing it. Each person who gave a compliment about the fish thought he was giving him praise, but in reality the person was causing distress.

Find things not always seen. Appreciate the small things. Try to think of something other than the obvious. A beautiful child knows he or she's beautiful and probably has been told so a million times. Try to come up with something else—compliment charm, wit, common sense, ability to play with others, sense of humor, athletic success, following orders, self-reliance, eating habits, making good choices, spiritual attributes, helpfulness, or intelligence. Pick something that will surprise and please the child.

One of the best sources to find compliments comes from movies. If you hear one you like write it down. Make a list. Find the right moment to use them. There are many unique heartfelt compliments found there. Look for ones that touch emotions, causing feelings to emerge. These are compliments that will always be remembered by all.

Back Up What You Say

You can strengthen your compliment by backing it up with some proof. For example, you could say, "That picture you made for me is wonderful. The colors are so bright and cheerful. I am so glad you picked my favorite color red; it makes me happy when I see your picture."

By telling the child what you specifically like about her picture, he or she is more likely to feel great about the compliment you just gave him or her. A specific compliment that is backed up will raise the self-esteem of the person with whom you're speaking.

By using creative and unusual words instead of everyday ones, you will give the compliment more importance and it will have longer staying-power with the individual.

Your dog sure loves you. I bet he wags his tail every time he sees you. You must be a good friend and owner to him. He looks so healthy and happy. Many children don't know how to be a great pet owner, but you sure must be. You are so kind and patient with him. You have the qualities of being a wonderful veterinarian.

Another example:

> "I love your new dress. It is so radiant and eye catching.
> The fabric has the appearance of fine silk. It seems to
> shine brighter than the stars. But the best part is it
> brings out the beauty and color of your eyes."

Now each time she wears the dress, she will remember the compliment from you, and you'll definitely remain in her good graces, for giving such a personalized compliment is out of this world! A point to consider is this compliment example highlights her appearance, which for most girls is primary in their self-evaluation. That can be a sole desire of a girl, but is not the point of this compliment. The compliment could have been about a picture, solving a puzzle, helping someone, or any other action. The example of the choice of her clothing just demonstrates to go beyond the first level of recognition and expand why you liked it and not necessarily relating to her appearance. As with the compliment to the dog owner, everytime he sees the dog wag his tail he will remember I am good with animals.

Don't Just Stop There

Remember, whenever you give compliments, they usually only last a few moments before the conversation moves on to another subject. If you want to really give a child a lift, give a great compliment and then continue to talk about it.

This is not to say that you need to drag on a conversation about a perfect school project or a special achievement to the point of embarrassment for the child. But you can reinforce your compliment by asking a question afterward. For example, you could say, "Your school project looks great, Ladd. It's really detailed, and it is so clean looking. Your hard work has paid off. I would definitely give you an A+ or higher. It is amazing how you got all the information in such a small area. What's your secret?"

Ladd will likely be only too happy to share his project's skill secrets. Your compliment will make him feel great and likely lead to a detailed conversation about his project that will leave both of you in high spirits.

Avoid Compliments That Use A Comparison Or Value Judgment

When in doubt about whether a compliment is a comparison or value judgment, think about this: a linking verb (a to-be verb such as *are*) is usually an indication of a comparison or value judgment. "You are the most beautiful"; "That piano playing was best of all"; "You have the prettiest smile, much better than all the rest." And definitely stay away from comparative words like *more, better, best,* and so on.

Now this only applies to comparing them to others in the family or close friends. Otherwise, what the heck, tell them that they are the best! Do all the comparisons you want—after all these are your grandchildren you are talking about.

People who find it hard to take compliments will usually deny these claims. This may be because they are underrating themselves or because they think you are overrating them! They might even get insulted. They may actually feel justified in denying your claims if, for instance, they feel that they didn't play the piano well. In their minds, they may be thinking, "Oh, Grandpa, you are just saying that, but you really don't mean it." Don't worry, it still feels good.

Be Patient

Giving the perfect compliment is also about waiting for the perfect moment. One thing you should avoid is trying to manufacture that moment. Timing is everything. Don't compliment someone on a task from a month ago, but at the time they finish. Remember, the compliment is for the other person at the appropriate time. The reason for the compliment is to bolster their ego, not yours. If done at the wrong time, it may be perceived as self-seeking and makes the giving more about you than the recipient.

Flattery and puffery have a place and can have the giver's best interests at heart. At the same time, waiting too long can mean the compliment loses its timeliness. Strive to strike a balance, focusing on the needs and timing of the recipient.

In *Groundhog Day*, a movie about a man who keeps living the same day over and over, the man would have one great day with a woman he was wooing, during which, he offered some spontaneous, meaningful compliments that she responded to in full appreciation. But when he tried the next day to recreate the same scenario, it didn't work and bombed horribly for him. You can't plan spontaneity. You can't *fully* preplan sincere compliments. You just have to be prepared to express your thoughts at the right time and in the right way to give the complete effect of your words.

Knowing how and when to give compliments to your grandkids is a great skill to have. By developing it, you can only improve your social and parenting talents. The best result comes through giving compliments that express your admiration.

Be Brief

It's easy to start rambling when you say something nice about someone. Don't linger around looking for a thank-you or feel the need to repeat yourself or venture beyond the confines of the compliment. This is especially true if you're moved to compliment a stranger. Breeze in, offer your heartfelt words, and jump right back into life ongoing.

Ask A Question With Your Compliment

If you want to use it as an opening to a discussion, ask a question about the subject of your compliment:

> That book is fun, and it has such big words designed for older children; you must be very smart to be able to read it. You are growing up so fast. Where did you get the book?

Other questions to add at the end of a compliment:

> How did you do that?
> What made you think of that?
> Why did you do it that way?
> Which was your favorite?
> How did that make you feel?

Be Yourself

You don't need to copy other folks' compliments all the time. These can have an air of phoniness, easily detected by children. Learn to develop your own words, thoughts, and feelings. You can get ideas and a rough structure of good compliments from this book, along from other sources, but you have to personalize the words and thoughts to every individual situation. After some practice, you will gain self-confidence, which is the key to delivering meaningful compliments.

Allow for Humor

Sometimes, a little humor never hurts, like the one grandpa who said, "I just do whatever Grandma [referring to his wife] tells me to do, and all is well. Just ask her." There are times, as grandfathers, when it is okay to use sarcastic humor with backhanded compliments. This is a fine line to walk, but if you have the right relationship with your grandchildren, this is not only appropriate, it is fun for both. The type of compliment this falls under comes out more like a tease or playfulness with your grandchildren.

"You throw like a girl."

Child's response: "Grandpa, I am a girl."

"You are the smartest and most handsome of all my ten-year-old grandsons."

Child's response: "Grandpa, I am your only ten-year-old grandson."

James Gooch

Practice, Practice, Practice

> *For some, paying a compliment is like a tightfisted miser*
> *going to the bank to make a withdrawal.*
>
> —Grandpa G

If you are not sure how to get started, begin by making a list of one-word compliments and using them as often as possible with your children and grandchildren. Examples:

athletic	funny	imaginative	reliable
brave	generous	kind	smart
bright	giving	nice	thankful
dependable	handsome	outgoing	wonderful
energetic	happy	patient	talented
focused	honest	pretty	

Write them down, make a checklist, and each time you use the word, put a mark next to it. Before long you will begin to do it naturally, without thinking about it.

While we were talking, Grandpa G described a trip he took with one of his friends to a convention. They had been discussing how hard it was to give compliments to those around them. They felt they should find a method to help them develop a way to overcome the fear of praising others, especially total strangers. They decided to make it a challenge, betting each other on who could give out the most sincere compliments during the week of their trip. Each would tally up their total compliments at the end of each day, and the winner would be paid: no cheating.

> When we started the trip, we were nervous about our bet, because neither one of us was good at talking to people and finding complimentary things to say. But we are both very competitive and didn't want to lose the bet.
>
> When we would stop at a store, we would try to find something to say, both of us thinking these people were going to consider us crazy for saying something stupid.

So our first attempts would be something to the tune of "Thanks, I appreciate your help," or a really daring one like, "Nice shirt."

Even though the first few attempts were pretty lame, we did notice people were responding very positively. As we continued to give more compliments, our fear left us, and gracious or admiring things became easier to utter at every opportunity.

We discovered that the more specific the comments, the better the response to our compliments. We would make remarks, such as "You must be really good for the company to trust you with so much responsibility"; "I bet your customers really like you. I can see why with your engaging and beautiful smile and your impressive knowledge."

We would talk to sales and checkout clerks, waiters, servers, other customers, and just random people on the street.

It was amazing how many people opened up to us. I think we were the only ones who ever gave some of those people a compliment in a whole day. If you consider that most people at work go all day without someone saying something nice to them, other than maybe a thank-you. Nobody takes the time to visit or exchange friendly conversation or, heaven forbid, show appreciation. It was fun talking to everyone. People would go out of their way to help us just because we were nice and showed some appreciation for them. By the time we reached the convention, we were seasoned veterans with regard to talking to people and praising everyone.

We continued our bet throughout the convention. By the end, we had made more true friends than anyone else. Wherever we went, we had people wanting to accompany us. To this day, we enjoy our contact with the close friends we made at the convention, including many that live in several other states and Canada. We made lifelong friends, all from sharing a few sincere compliments.

My impression is that the majority of compliments given and received in this world are earnest and well intentioned. I like to think of them as tiny, self-generated miracles. Never underestimate the transformative power of a compliment, my fellow grandpas. Just about every time you tell another human being, "Hey! I like you, and I like what you're doing," you're changing that person's life for the better, even if they don't yet realize it. Every time you muster up the courage to praise another person, you're doing the world a service by bolstering that person's confidence and self-esteem.

Catching Children Being Good

> *The definition of a compliment is catching and praising someone in the act of being good.*
>
> —Grandpa G

There is an old-time technique on how to teach children to be quiet when a person is on the phone. The secret is to catch the child playing quietly during a phone call, then immediately afterward tell the child how proud you are of him or her and thank the child for staying so quiet while you were talking on the phone. Usually children are totally surprised by your comment. They were completely unaware of you being on the phone. It only takes two or three times of positive reinforcement, praising them, for a pattern to emerge in their mind that keeping quiet during the phone call is a good thing and generates praise.

In an episode of a famous TV series, *The Big Bang Theory*, one roommate offered chocolate to his roommate's girlfriend each time she did something to conform to his desired way of thinking. After awhile, she changed her pattern—how she talked, where she sat, and various other behaviors. Each time she responded to his wishes, he would offer her a chocolate; she never realized she was responding to a positive-reinforcement technique of praise-and-reward. Even though it was used in a humorous setting, the truth is praise-and-reward does have a desired result. She was rewarded for being good.

Children, in particular teens, often hear negative comments on a daily basis. "Why didn't you take the garbage out?" "You left your room a mess." "I can't believe you forgot your book at school." "Do you realize that is the third pair of shoes you have lost?"

Don't get caught in this pattern; you need to balance negative feedback with positive statements. *Catch* your grandchild *doing something well* and leave a complimentary note, a card, or letter for them to see or read. The power of a written message has four times the impact as a verbal one. Things on refrigerators or walls are like trophies to a child. Even when they do mundane, everyday simple tasks, it matters to them when you praise them. A mere note may read, "Thanks for putting your dishes in the dishwasher without being told," or "I was excited to see your math-test grade. Way to go!"

One grandfather was telling me about his grandchildren: "I have the best grandchildren. They come over to my house and mow my lawn, clean the yard, trim the hedge, and sweep the back porch without ever being asked or paid. They just do it on their own," he said.

However, I know this grandfather: he never passes up the opportunity to talk about his grandchildren and how much he appreciates them. He praises them all the time. He tells them constantly how great they are, thanking them for the things they do for him and his wife. They are always receiving compliments from him. For them, it is a pleasure to do those chores, because they are being fed with good feelings of appreciation, recognition, and satisfaction.

Other ways to show appreciation is by writing notes to them on cards, giving presents, texting, and e-mail. Positive, complimentary notes give young children and teens the positive feedback they need. At the same time, you may be teaching by demonstration how to give compliments to others, a valuable skill in building their friendships.

Go Public

All children want to be praised in front of others. Not excessively, but pointing something positive out in front of family, friends, and neighbors will please the child mightily and show your affection for the child. You may have to be careful with this if you have very shy grandchildren, though. You don't want to make them feel self-conscious. (But remember, even to a shy child, it still feels good, and they love it.)

A whole industry was created with bumper stickers praising children, "My child is an Honor Student at _____ School." Award ceremonies, plaques, ribbons, trophies are all examples of showing compliments of a child in public.

Note: Praising someone in front of others with a compliment has four times the impact than one said in private.

Remember, It Feels Good

An enjoyable compliment is like an ice-cold drink to a parched mouth in the middle of the Arizona summer desert. It tastes and feels so good. Often, a person will know that the compliment is just flattery to say something nice. But, it still feels good.

A woman from the survey gave me this example:

> One time, when I was a teenager, I was recovering from a long illness and still had the look of death warmed over. I looked pale and very white. I didn't feel good and was worried about my appearance and being seen by my friends. Our family was going to church for the first time after my sickness, to support my younger brother who was doing a play, and he wanted us all to be there, especially me. I was nervous, so I asked Grandpa how I looked. He stopped and began slowly turning me around.
>
> "Girl, you look fabulous; your hair is perfect, your eyes sparkle like glitter, your dress is gorgeous, and your face is beaming with enthusiasm. You are beautiful. I am

going to have to beat the boys away from you today," he responded.

Now, I know it wasn't true. But it felt so good. It was what I needed to hear in order to walk out that door. I understand he could have told me the truth, saying something to the tune of "What do you expect? You have been sick for a long time. You can't presume you would look good, but people will be nice to you when they find out what you have been through." But he didn't, and I always loved him for that.

Everyone likes to have nice things said to them. Even when they know the words may be untrue, as long as the one saying the praise is doing so with real intent. The attention still feels good.

"Oh, Grandpa, you are just saying that."

To some grandfathers, these are their favorite words to hear from a child.

Children crave attention from adults. It represents acceptance and value to them. How often have we heard children yell to us, "Grandpa, watch this," "Grandpa, listen to me," or "Grandpa, play with me"?

This is their way of telling you they want attention and recognition from you.

Grandpa G gave me another example he uses with his grandchildren:

Every time I visit my grandchildren in whatever city they live, I will ask them a question.

"You know what I heard today?" I will ask.

"No, what?" they respond.

"I heard that the _____ [I insert their last name, their family name] kids are the best in _____ [I insert their town, city or state]."

"Really, Grandpa?" they question.

"Yes, that's what I heard," I say.

Now do they believe it? Maybe for the first few times, yes, but after awhile, it is more of a game. Now they will respond with, "We know, Grandpa. The _____s are the best kids in _____."

The point is still the same. Do they know the statement is probably untrue? Yes, but it still feels good to them (because they know I think that), and it gives them special attention with a positive statement.

One additional statement came from a woman telling me about her grandfather and how he treated her grandmother. This was listed under the items most remembered about their grandfather.

I noticed a pattern my grandfather would do each time we would go into a gathering of people. He would stop and look around the room, checking everyone out, then turn to my grandmother and whisper, "Yep, you are the prettiest woman in the room," he would say.

She would always respond, "You are just saying that. Look at all the younger women."

He would say, "In my eyes, to me, you are the prettiest woman in the room."

I know Grandma wasn't the most beautiful, and Grandpa was just saying it to make Grandma feel good, but Grandma never got tired of his admiration and attention. Her face would light up every time he said it.

Always remember *all compliments feel good.* If someone pushes back to negate the compliment, don't get discouraged, because in their heart they still like it. Don't ever stop praising those around you.

Remember the one who constantly gives compliments and praises to those around him is the healthy one. The one who pushes back when he or she receives compliments is the unhealthy person.

Words of Caution

Watch out for compliments that could do more damage than good, like "You'll look so great when you finally get those braces off." This a big no-no.

Avoid sarcasm and smirking, especially when you're giving compliments that seem sincere; it can have a negative effect.

Avoid complimenting a child in order to get them to do something for you. Children are smart. It doesn't take them long to figure out the motive of your praising.

Don't compliment them too frequently or too rarely. Use good judgment, because either will bring a question in their mind of how sincere you are toward them.

Compliments show others how we feel, that we care about them, and that we want to make them happy.

Chapter 12

Be Real and Truthful Or What Can Grandpa Do to Help the Grandchildren Develop a Healthy View of Themselves?

The greatest reward is helping a person realize he is of great worth in this world.

—Grandpa G

Think About What You Want To Say Before You Say It

Children can be sensitive to the words from parents, grandparents, and others. Remember to praise your child not only for a job well done, but also for effort. Try to be truthful. For example, if your grandchild doesn't make the soccer team, avoid saying something like, "Well, next time you'll have to work harder in order to make it." Instead, say something like, "Well, you didn't make the team, but I'm really proud of the effort you put into it." Concentrate on effort, instead of outcome. Using warmth and humor can help your grandkids learn about themselves and appreciate what makes them unique.

Sometimes, a child's skill level is just not there. Helping kids overcome failures or disappointments can better equip them to learn what they're good at and what they're not so good at. Recognize some things you can change and some things you can't. If you recognize what there is about the child that you can influence enough to change, then start today. If it's something you can't change (like size or physical limitations), then start to work toward loving them the way they are.

Grandpa G to a grandson: "Remember that there are things about yourself you can't change. You should accept and love these things—such as skin color, height, color of your eyes, and shoe size—because they are part of you. You have your own uniqueness, different from anyone else. Embrace it, develop it, and enjoy it."

Grandpa is a strong, positive role model. Often, we as adults will say things like, "I can't swing a bat either" or "I couldn't kick a ball to save my life," but it's important to be positive when thinking or talking about yourself as well. It's good to share your weaknesses, but don't allow yourself to be excessively harsh, pessimistic, or unrealistic about your abilities and limitations in front of your grandchildren. Your grandchildren see and hear you. Children are great imitators. They might eventually do what you do.

Work On Your Own Self-Esteem, And They'll Have A Great Role Model

If you're used to focusing on your shortcomings, start thinking about positive aspects of yourself that outweigh them. When you catch yourself being too critical, counter it by saying something positive about yourself. Teach by doing for yourself, especially in front of your grandchildren. If you are positive, they will be positive. If you are negative, then they will be negative. How you see yourself can be passed down to younger generations as what is acceptable behavior for them.

Teach Your Grandchildren Emotional Coping Skills

Grandpa G has what he calls a *Get Me Out of Depression* book. He said that he came up with the idea while playing Monopoly, when he got a get-out-of-jail card. He thought, *Wouldn't it be nice to have different cards to help us get out of trouble when faced with difficulties?* That's when he came up with the idea of a get-me-out-of-depression book. I asked him about it. Here is what is inside his book.

> Starting with my family, I inserted several pictures I like about each of them, often relating to a pleasant event, something to jog a good memory. Then I expanded the pictures to include my friends. While thinking of them, I recorded my feelings about each person and what they meant to me on paper. Next, I began writing stories of positive experiences with each of them. I wrote about funny events, challenging experiences, and meaningful incidents that I cherish.
>
> After that, I created a detailed list of all the things I am grateful for in my life—family, home, health, job, friends, religion, and so on. I finished it with inspirational thoughts, poems, and sayings that bolster and uplift my spirit, touching my soul. I also inserted a list of friends to call. If I do call them, I will bring up an old event we shared together reminding me of better times. I have found, in doing so, it forces me to relive those lost feelings and puts me in a better mood. By the time I finish reading from my *Get Me Out of Depression* book, I always feel better and more empowered to face the next challenge in my life.

Since I talked to Grandpa G, I not only created a *Get Me Out of Depression* book for myself but have one for our family. If someone is down, I will refer to the stories and good experiences from the past. Doing this in a subtle way can make a huge difference in the mood of the family member.

It is good, Grandpa, to view mistakes as learning opportunities. Learn to accept that children will make mistakes, because everyone does. Mistakes are part of learning. Remind yourself that a person's talents are constantly developing, and everyone excels at different things. Thank goodness, because this is what makes people interesting.

Help Children See Correct Versus Incorrect Beliefs About Themselves

It's critical for grandparents to identify children's irrational beliefs about themselves. Children at birth come with self-reliance and self-trust. To change those attributes, they must develop a learned behavior. If we have been treated with mistrust since childhood, we have learned to not trust our own feelings. Unfortunately, such a pattern may be passed on from one generation to the next. Those who have developed a consistent habit of needing someone else's advice at times when emotions are on the line do not develop the ability to act for themselves. They are constantly seeking a vote of confidence from others, instead of finding from it within themselves. Often they get caught up worrying about perfection, attractiveness, ability, or trying to avoid anything challenging.

Some grandparents and parents paralyze their children by demanding perfection, instead of allowing the child to move forward even if not perfect.

This can hamper a child's ability to try new or challenging things, maybe second-guessing potential success by creating negative thoughts like, "I won't audition for the play until I lose ten pounds" or "I won't try out for the team until I am a better player." Instead, we should encourage children to think about what they are good at, what they enjoy, and to just go for it.

Grandparents can be very effective at helping children set more accurate standards and be more realistic in evaluating themselves. This will help them have a healthy self-perspective and self-awareness.

Another time, Grandpa G was giving advice to one of his grandchildren, he said, "Remember that your body is your own, no matter what shape, size, or complexion it is. If you are worried about your weight or size, we can check with the doctor to make sure you're healthy. Remind yourself of things about your body that are cool, like 'My legs are strong; I have great eyesight; my hearing is top-notch; and I can skate really well.'"

If children have inaccurate perceptions of themselves, these perceptions can take root and become reality to them as they grow up. For example, a child who does very well in school but struggles with science might say, "I can't do science. I'm a bad student." This belief sets the child up for failure. Focusing on one item can change the whole self-evaluation. Encourage children to see a situation in a more objective way. A helpful response might be: "You are a *good* student. You do great in school. Science is a subject that is hard to understand for many people. Maybe I can work on it with you."

Grandpa G, again talking to his grandchild: "When you hear negative comments in your head, tell yourself to stop. Remind yourself of things you're good at, and if you can't think of anything, ask someone else! You can also learn a new skill (for example, karate, dance, fishing, hunting, working with animals, a musical instrument, or computers) so you can feel great about that!"

Grandpa G explained how he talked to his grandchildren concerning a method to help them become comfortable with themselves:

> Don't just say, "I'm great." Be specific when referring to something good about yourself, like, "I was a good friend to John today" or "I did better on that test than I thought I would." Find small things that make you feel good about yourself.
>
> Make a list of the stuff you're good at doing. It can be anything from drawing or singing to playing a sport or telling a good joke. If you're having trouble with your list, ask your mom or dad to help you with it. Then add a few things to the list that you'd *like* to be good at. Your mom or dad can help you plan a way to work on those skills or talents.
>
> In addition, before you go to bed every night, list three things in your day that really made you happy or that you feel thankful for. Post it on the refrigerator or in your room where you can see it every day. Just remind yourself how terrific of a person you are. And always remember, Grandpa G loves you and believes in you.

Focus On What Is Achieved Rather Than On Being Perfect

Grandpa, be positive, especially when giving truthful feedback. Saying comments like "You always work yourself up into such a frenzy!" will make a child feel as though they have no control over their outbursts. I recommend a little different approach, such as, "I can see you were very angry with your brother, but it was nice that you were able to talk about it instead of yelling or hitting." This acknowledges a child's feelings, rewards the choice made, and encourages the child to make the right choice again next time.

Helping Children To Try New Things Creates Self-Confidence

Experiments with different activities will help them get in touch with their talents. It develops confidence in facing a new challenge. Then take pride in watching them learn new skills, constantly telling them about your happiness in their skills.

Reward Them With Spontaneous Affectionate

Give hugs and tell grandchildren you're proud of them when you can see them putting effort toward something or trying something at which they previously failed. Your love will help boost your grandchild's self-esteem. Write cards and letters expressing how much you appreciate them. Just don't overdo it.

Help Children Find Service Projects

Service projects allow children to feel good about themselves by helping others. A child will always want to please. All people, adults and children, often get caught up in their own world and desires. When they focus too much on themselves and not enough on the needs of other people, they lose the ability to fit in. But when they stop thinking about themselves and concentrate on the contribution they could make to the rest of the world, they don't worry as much about their own flaws. This increases self-confidence and allows them to contribute with maximum efficiency.

The more they contribute to the world, the more they will be rewarded with personal success and recognition. Find projects like these:

- helping to clean up their neighborhood
- participating in a walkathon for a good cause
- helping teach younger children a skill
- volunteering time in some additional way of serving others, even it is within their own family

Volunteering and contributing to the local community can have positive effects on self-esteem for everyone involved. When children feel like they are making a difference and that their help is valued, it does wonders to improve their self-worth.

Provide A Safe, Loving Home Environment

Children who don't feel safe or are abused at home are at greater risk for developing poor self-esteem. A child who is exposed to parents or grandparents who fight and argue repeatedly may feel he has no control over his environment and becomes helpless or depressed. Hopefully, this doesn't exist in the home of your grandchildren. If you provide a place of peace and refuge, it will enhance their self-worth and self-being.

Show Grandchildren How To Set Goals

Have them think about what they would like to accomplish, then make a plan for how to do it. Teach them how to stick with their plan and keep track of their progress.

One young lady told me about how her grandpa had set up a master planner for all his grandchildren in his office.

> Grandpa had a giant calendar on his wall with all the months for the whole year listed. Each year the grandchildren would put items on the calendar that related to them individually. We each were assigned our own color so we could quickly follow our individual events. Birthdays, activities, school events, sports teams, games, clubs, music recitals, campouts, and all items of

interest found their way to the calendar. He would also have each of us put goals, achievements, and things we wanted to do during the year on our planners. The calendar was always being updated and changing.

I would look forward to going to Grandpa's house just to see the calendar. It was fun to see what my cousins were doing. Of course, it felt good to see my name and activities upon the calendar.

Teach your grandchildren to *exercise, exercise, exercise!*

Exercise relieves stress and helps you to be healthier and happier. Along the same lines as personal appearance, physical fitness has a huge effect on self-confidence. If a child is out of shape, the child will feel insecure, unattractive, and less energetic. By working out, children can improve their physical appearance, energize themselves, and accomplish something positive.

One of the easiest ways to tell how a child feels about himself or herself is to examine the child's way of walking. Is it slow? Tired? Painful? Or is it energetic and purposeful? Children with confidence walk quickly. They have places to go, people to see, and important work to do. Even if they aren't in a hurry, they can increase their self-confidence by putting some *pep in their step.*

Having the discipline to work out not only makes them feel better, it creates positive momentum that they can build on each day. Go with them on a walk, set the stage, and create a goal for exercising.

Grandpa G shared with me how he used to help children get some exercise.

Whenever I visit with my grandchildren, we will always go on walks together. I always try to make it as interesting as I can. Sometimes we count certain colors of homes or types of trees. Other times, we bark at dogs to see if we can get a response. But always, we talk about anything that is of interest to them. Many times, I tell

> them stories about the family. Walking has a calming effect and builds a better relationship.
>
> On different occasions, I will challenge my grandchildren to see how many push-ups or sit-ups they can do. I mark it down on a calendar with dates attached. Children love to see everyone's score. Again, it is an unsuspecting way to get children to do something good for themselves.

Work At Helping Them Develop Good Posture

Generally, the way a person carries him or herself tells a story. People with slumped shoulders and lethargic movements display a lack of self-confidence. They aren't enthusiastic about what they're doing, and they don't consider themselves important. By practicing good posture, they will automatically feel more confident. Teach your grandkids to stand up straight, keep their heads up, and make eye contact. Make a game of it. These are all techniques used by many organizations to boost achievement (military training, sales classes, positive-thinking seminars, etc.). A child with good posture will make a positive impression on others and instantly feel more alert and empowered.

Grandpa, Most Important, Have Fun

Show the children how to have fun while doing projects that build self-esteem. Explain to them how it is enjoyable to spend time with the people they care about and doing the things they love. Help them to relax and have a good time. Introduce music while working, make up games to take away the *it-sounds-like-work-to-me* syndrome. Reward good work with snacks or a trip to the local convenience store.

> *A grandpa's job is to help the grandchildren get into mischief they haven't thought of yet.*
>
> —Grandpa G

In conclusion, developing strong self-worth should be a very big part of growing up. As children get older and face tough decisions, especially under peer pressure, the higher their self-esteem, the better they can make good decisions. It's important that they like and respect themselves.

When promoting healthy self-esteem, make sure your grandchildren don't end up feeling that if they are average or normal at something, it's the same as not being good or special. Excellence is something to strive for, but it's not a measure of your worth. You have value just by being alive. All the tools listed here were developed to help your grandchildren cultivate a strong, healthy self-esteem.

Chapter 13

The Insanity of Communication

The single biggest problem with communication is the illusion that it has taken place.

—George Bernard Shaw

A grandfather was reading Bible stories from the Book of Genesis to his young grandson.

He read, "The man named Lot was warned to take his wife and flee out of the city, but his wife looked back and was turned to salt."

His grandson asked, "What happened to the flea?"

Proper communication is what makes the world go around. If the communication is not correctly sent and received, then problems will happen. Bad communication in business can lead to loss or failure; in the international arena, missed communication can lead to war; in personal relationships, poor communications can lead to destruction of the relationship.

Communication comprises the building blocks of our relationships. It is through communication that we convey our thoughts, feelings, and connection to one another.

Developing good communication skills is critical for successful relationships, whether the grandparent, parent, child, spouse, or sibling relationship. All of us have had experiences when we felt our message was heard and understood. On the other side, we've all had experiences when we felt misunderstood and even ignored.

Generally, when we are heard, we feel good, we are less angry or stressed, and more open to resolving problems than when we feel misunderstood. For grandchildren, developing their communication skills, frustration can be very real when they aren't understood. Knowing that one is heard and correctly understood helps to develop trust and caring between people.

How we say the words is as important as the words themselves. When one hears a word, it doesn't always translate to the meaning behind them. Let's take the following phrase, "I didn't say you eat fish." If you break it down and emphasize each word separately the phrase has several different meanings. Yet a foreign student of the language would not catch all the meanings.

I didn't say you eat fish. Implies it was someone else who said it.

I *didn't* say you eat fish. Implies the person denies saying it.

I didn't *say* you eat fish. Implies he didn't say that but something else.

I didn't say *you* eat fish. Implies the statement was about someone else eating fish.

I didn't say you *eat* fish. Implies you don't eat fish, but do something else with them, maybe just fish for them.

I didn't say you eat *fish.* Implies you eat something different.

Another example would be if asked the question, "Would you want a *hot* computer?"

One person might say yes, thinking the computer is trendy, fantastically performing, and great looking. While a second person might say no, thinking it was stolen. A third could think it was physically hot, and not wanting it because of the possibility of getting burned when touching it.

How words are presented is only a small part of relaying the true message trying to be conveyed.

A grandfather told me of his experience when visiting his grandson's school for show-and-tell. He was a carpenter by profession and said he brought his tools to school to show

how to hammer a nail, cut wood, and sand to create a smooth finish. Because of the children's young age, he tried to keep it simple for them. After he finished with what he thought was a masterful presentation, he asked if there were any questions. One boy in the front row raised his hand.

The grandfather pointed to him, expecting a question about the tools, and received instead, "Are your eyes blue?"

With children you never know what is being communicated or if they are listening.

The power of nonverbal communication cannot be underestimated. Messages we send through our posture, gestures, facial expression, and spatial distance are said to account for over half what is perceived and understood by others. In fact, through our body language, we are always communicating, whether we want to or not!

In his book *Silent Messages*, Dr. Albert Mehrabian has provided a breakdown of the process of communication. Here were the most common results:

> 55% = Nonverbal (smiles, shrugs, gestures, facial
> expressions, etc.)
> 38% = Tone of voice (questioning, laughing, crying, high,
> low, loud, etc.)
> 7% = Words

As you can see, nonverbal messages are the primary way that we communicate emotions. In fact, nonverbal body-language is the single, most important way of communicating.

Facial expression: The face is perhaps the most important conveyor of emotional information. A face can light up with enthusiasm, energy, desire, or approval, or darken with confusion, boredom, and displeasure. The eyes are particularly expressive in conveying feelings of joy, sadness, anger, or confusion. In children, you can often almost read their thoughts in their faces. On the reverse side, children can see us at a more basic level, without us realizing their better understanding of our true emotions, for all is simple to them.

Postures and gestures: Our body postures can create a feeling of warm openness or cold rejection. For example, when a grandchild faces us, sitting quietly with hands loosely folded in the lap, a feeling of anticipation and interest is apparent. If the child is in a constant state of movement, it implies impatience or nervousness. A posture of arms crossed on the chest portrays a feeling of inflexibility. How often are adults communicating that to children? A downwardly hung head with no eye contact may mean fear or guilt. The action of gathering up one's possessions can signal a desire to end the conversation or contact.

Another form of communication is transmitted through pitch, tone, and speed of our voices. Basically, *how we say something,* rather than *what we say* accounts for approximately 38 percent of what is communicated to someone. A sentence can convey entirely different meanings depending on the emphasis on words and the tone of voice. Some points to remember about this form of sending a message:

- When we are angry or excited, our speech tends to become more rapid and higher pitched.
- When we are bored, feeling down (or raised in the South), our speech tends to be slower. It can even become a monotone.
- We can be very abrupt or silent when we feel defensive.

We see examples constantly of nonverbal communication—when individuals will say one thing with actions that relate a totally different meaning. Grandchildren often speak louder in action than in words. Their facial expressions and tones of voice are greatly enhanced while trying to convey their messages. An example would be the following.

A granddaughter slams the door. Grandpa asks, "Is there something wrong?" Answer: "No, everything is just peachy."

Obviously, the words would indicate all is okay, but the meaning, given by tone, is quite different. We as grandfathers have to listen carefully to catch the meaning, not just the words. Words by themselves have one meaning, but with tone, it is different, especially if it's a sarcastic tone:

"Really."	"Everything is just fine."
"If you say so."	"No, I am not mad."
"Maybe."	"I would *love* to help
"We will see."	my brother."

In all of our communications, we want to strive to send consistent verbal and nonverbal messages. When our messages are inconsistent, the listener might become confused. Inconsistency can also create a lack of trust and undermine the chance to build a good working relationship.

If a message is conveyed with conflicting verbal and nonverbal information, the nonverbal information tends to be what is believed. Which would you believe more? Your wife tells you she is not mad, but she has hard eyes, a stern voice, and tight jaws? Do you believe the body or the words? Hmm . . . ? Obviously, she's mad.

Each day, we interact with family members who have different opinions, values, beliefs, and needs than our own. We are often put in situations with grandchildren to try to answer difficult questions and provide intuitive advice. Our ability to exchange ideas with them, understand their points of view, help them find solutions to their problems and successfully create a positive meeting of the minds can be enriched by utilizing the steps and processes presented in this book. Doing so will significantly improve our effectiveness in communicating with our grandchildren and other members of the family.

Let me say again, the act of communicating involves verbal and nonverbal components. The verbal component refers to the content of our message, the choice and arrangement of our words. The nonverbal component refers to the message we send through our body language and how we say what we say—the tone, speed, and volume of our voices.

With little children who are developing their verbal communication skills, there are no hidden meanings; they are open and straightforward in their earnest desire to communicate. There are no preplanned speeches; they just say what they think. What words, tone, and physical expressions they do understand are all incorporated in making the point they are trying to express. Their whole body radiates what they want to say. The high level of complex speech has not been developed yet, but comes later, over time. Both good and bad communication is a learned, complicated system after years of exposure.

Grandpa G tells me of his pleasure in really listening to little ones:

> I have learned to listen close to young children, not only to understand their words, but to honor their overwhelming desire to achieve the meeting of the minds. It is so much fun to watch and hear the speech patterns they use. You never have to guess what they want or feel, because they will tell you very pointedly. They present their moods with their bodies, voices, and words such as:
>
> *Excitement*—jumping up and down, in high pitch, screaming, "Grandpa, Grandpa, I saw the biggest bug outside!"
>
> *Sadness*—a pouting face, head down, teary-eyed, almost moaning, "My brother won't let me play with him."
>
> *Happiness*—a big smile, wide eyes, joyful face, bright voice, "Grandpa, I love the *chocolate ice cream*! It is my favorite."

It is so refreshing to talk to children, their uninhibited utterances are straightforward without prethought, political correctness, worries of what others will think, or fear of consequences. With little children, you always know where you stand and what they are truly thinking. It is too bad we, as adults, have lost the innocence of honest communication with each other.

Young children are the only ones who can get away with noticing and mentioning personal observations like, "Grandpa, how come you have such a big belly?" "Grandma, why do you have gray hair?" "Grandma, why do you have so many wrinkles?" or "Grandpa, you have hair in your ears."

Children say what they see, think, and feel. There is a sweet innocence in stating the obvious. The classic tale of "The Emperor's New Clothes," by Hans Christian Andersen, illustrates this with the perfect example. Wouldn't it be nice on occasion to live in a society while peering through the eyes of an innocent child?

There is a story about a grandpa and his little granddaughter standing together, looking in a mirror. This is their conversation.

> "Grandpa, how come you are so old and wrinkly?" she asked.
>
> "Because God made me that way," he responded.
>
> After staring at him a few moments, then looking at herself, she said, "Thank goodness God had gotten better at it when he made me."

As children grow, so does their use of words, expressions, and meanings. They learn how to hide, weave the truth, and manipulate for their benefit. Society provides opportunity to acquire techniques in communication from many sources—movies, school grounds, TV, friends, and family. With age, their ability to develop and become more skilled in controlling their speech patterns increases. By the time children become young adults, the innocence is long gone. They understand the advantages of mastering verbal speech, tones, and body language while conveying their intentions. Delivering their presentation just like their elders, with stretched truths or honesty depending only on the desired results.

Chapter 14

Listen, Listen, Listen

A person who takes on the task to truly listen to our issues can influence our whole perspective and add unrealized understanding.

—Grandpa G

The key to receiving messages effectively is listening. Listening is a combination of hearing what another person says and psychological involvement with the person who is talking. The art of listening requires more than hearing words. It requires a *desire* to understand another person, an attitude of respect and acceptance, and a willingness to open our minds to see things from another's point of view. Listening requires a high level of concentration and energy. It demands that we set aside our own thoughts and agendas, put ourselves in another's shoes, and try to see the world through that person's eyes.

Grandpa G told me this story:

> One time, I was at home, deep in thought about a project I was working with, when my little three-year-old granddaughter came up and put both hands on the sides of my face. Moving her head to within three inches of my eyes, she said, "Grandpa, Grandpa, hello, are you in there?"

I then realized she had been asking me a question, but I had been lost in thought and didn't hear her.

Sometimes, we don't always focus on what folks are saying to us, thus comes the age-old question, "Are you listening to me?"

I don't believe a person can really hear anyone while doing something else at the same time.

Women of every age want to be heard. Remember, how women get their worth is through relationships; communication is a crucial part of a relationship.

One Grandpa explained how he loved to build model airplanes and fly them. He said he would spend hours working in his garage on his hobby, putting the airplanes together. It was his passion and relief valve. Often his wife and granddaughter would come out to the garage and try to get him to come inside and spend time with them. He said many times they would act as if they were jealous of the airplanes. "I think they thought they were in competition with the airplanes. If I didn't drop what I was doing and take part in their activity, later it would turn into a terrible argument."

He told me he learned from a friend that if he would spend at least thirty minutes a day of uninterrupted time talking and giving his attention to them, they would give him all the time he wanted to work with his airplanes. They just needed to be reassured of their importance to him.

What this grandfather discovered was that our loved ones want to be important in our lives. Someone who feels he or she is not important in a positive way will do things to become important in a negative way. Many relationships dissolve because one person doesn't seem to matter to the other person. When one person doesn't invest time in a relationship by listening, engaging, trying to understand the other, then a wall begins going up between them, so high that it may become impossible to be breached by either side. This has the potential for major relationship problems in the future. As grandfathers, we can't afford to have walls building between us and our grandchildren.

In the 1960s TV show, *All in the Family*, the main character, Archie Bunker, would often tell his wife, Edith, "Stifle yourself." Even though it was meant to be funny—and it was funny—there were hidden, suppressed feelings that surfaced over time as his wife eventually acquired her voice and opinions. In today's relationships, when a person does not give the time or make it safe for another to express his or her thoughts and views, it is seen to convey the message to "stifle yourself." The underlying feelings are *you don't think my opinion is important . . . my thoughts are of no value . . . you think I am inferior to you.*

One of the worst feelings a person can have is to be made to feel inferior. This quite often is felt by grandchildren. Not to be important enough or not to be allowed to contribute to the conversation can be very demeaning and hurtful. By not listening to a person, you are sending this message loud and clear, creating and reinforcing the self-evaluation of feeling inferior. Whether it be a wife, girlfriend, your children or grandchildren, you can't afford to not listen to them, to validate their importance to you. After all, you expect it of them.

Real listening requires that we suspend judgment, evaluation, and approval in an attempt to understand another's emotions, thoughts, and attitudes. Listening to understand can be a difficult task.

Grandpa G was talking about an experience he had with his granddaughter.

> We were going for a walk, which we often did in the evening. During the walk my granddaughter, who is thirteen, said, "I don't want to get married and have children."
>
> Now my first (over)reaction and thoughts were *What?! How can you say you don't want to get married? You are only thirteen; you still have years ahead of you to experience. There is no way you can possibly know how you will feel a few years from now!*
>
> Even though every fiber in body wanted to blurt out these words, I didn't, holding it inside. The reason for

my delayed response lay in the fact I had just finished a sales course of what was called active listening. We were taught that people don't always say what they really believe and will camouflage their true meaning with something else. So I decided to use some of the techniques on my granddaughter.

The formula is for you to repeat back what the person said in a question form. So I asked her, "You don't want to get married?"

She responded, "No, I don't want to get married so I won't have any children."

I asked her, "You don't want to have children?"

"No, I don't want to have children, because I wouldn't want to be like Mom," she said.

"Why don't you want to be like your mother?" I questioned.

"Then I would not have a child like Todd," she said.

"You wouldn't want a child like Todd?" I asked.

"He is such a pain," she recited.

"Why is he such a pain?" I asked.

"He will not let me use his iPod like he promised," she responded.

"You are unhappy because he changed his mind about letting you use his iPod?" I inquired.

"Yes, and I promised I would show it to two of my friends who are coming over, and now I don't know what I am going to do!" she exclaimed.

Grandpa G explained, "By listening and trying to understand her underlying meaning, not just the initial words, I was able to uncover the real problem that was bothering her. She was mad at her brother, and it had nothing to do with getting married."

Grandpa G had a lot patience to get to the bottom of his granddaughter's true problem. Mirroring a conversation sounds like it is downplaying what the child is saying, but in reality the repeating of someone's words need not be recognized as such, if it is done with sincerity. I have tried it with my family members, and the technique does work.

Sometimes, grandparents worry that if they listen attentively and patiently to a child who is saying something they disagree with, they are inadvertently sending a message of agreement. In order to set the correct perspective, we as grandparents want to jump in with our vast knowledge and experience to impart to our grandchildren solutions to solve their concerns. It is correct to say that our life experience, knowledge, and information could help the child, as is the feeling we could move them onto the right path. Our intentions are good. Our desire is usually one of protection and to prevent them from getting hurt. But sometimes grandchildren need to fail in order to grow and get stronger. Plus, most of the time, they can figure it out for themselves.

The key to giving advice is knowing the right time—*timing is everything.* Hear the child, and you will hear when your input is desired. Most children are self-reliant enough to distinguish what they need to heal themselves. Give them credit; they will ask you for information. You must withhold your desire to jump in telling them what you think they should do.

First, *don't* say anything; just listen. Stop and think: were you asked for advice or just to hear what the child is feeling? If advice is called for, it will be asked for.

One of the biggest mistakes a person can make when someone comes to him to talk about a problem is to give advice. This is a common mistake that men make. Men tend to be solution-oriented. A man gets paid to solve problems. All day at work, they find solutions. When a man hears a problem, he wants to figure out how to take care of it and solve it. Men in general, have a tendency to want to analyze the perceived problem, instead of trying to help lift the burden. In some cases, volunteering solutions and sound suggestions can be very valuable. However, most people do not want you to solve their problems, but instead to understand how they feel about the problem. How it is affecting their lives.

> *I always know when a child or my wife wants me to help*
> *them handle the problem with advice. They will ask for it.*
> *It is very simple; they use words such as: "Can you help*
> *me with this?" "What do you think about it?" "What would*
> *you do?" or "I need some advice." If they don't ask, then*
> don't *give any. Just listen.*
>
> —Grandpa G

I have found when individuals, old or young, are opening up and spilling out their hearts while in some agonizing emotion, it is probably the worst time to give advice. Most of the time, a person will come to his or her own wise choices or answers without my help. One grandpa was mentioning this observation while relating an experience with his wife. Even though it pertained to his wife and not his grandchildren, the principle still applies.

> I come home from work tired, and my wife meets me at the door. As soon as I walk in, she launches into a problem about her family, concerning her sister. Being a good husband, I listen for over an hour as she discussed the situation. When she got through, trying to help, I proceeded to give her what I thought were solutions. Did you try this or try that? I asked. I was coming up with great ideas and suggestions.
>
> Finally she said, with an attitude, "Fine, why don't you just go call her for me and handle the situation, since you seem so much better equipped to deal with it than I am?"
>
> She was very put out at me. Because of her response to me, I became mad. I thought, Here I sat listening to her tell me all about the problem; then when I started trying to help her, she got angry at me.
>
> We didn't talk for a two weeks.
>
> After many years, I have learned when she is telling me about a difficulty or situation from work, school, church, or family, she doesn't want for me to solve it, but for me to recognize how she felt under those

circumstances. She only wanted me to listen to her, for her to be able to express to me her pain. I guarantee you, in every case, she had already thought of every solution, analyzing extensively about the issue, long before she talked to me. She wasn't looking for a mouth, but a shoulder to lean on.

When people ask for advice, often they already know the solutions, but hoped or wished they didn't.

When we listen effectively, we gain information that is valuable to understanding the problem as the other person sees it, not just the solution. We gain a greater understanding of the other person's perception. After all, the truth is subjective and a matter of perception. When we have a deeper understanding of others' perceptions and feelings, whether we agree with the perception or share the feelings or not, we hold the key to understanding the others' motivation, attitude, and behavior. In most cases, those you care about want you to plainly understand what they are experiencing—to *share* their feelings and, often, their pain rather than to be left alone in them.

Grandpa G told me about an experience he had with his nine-year-old grandson after a dive meet.

> It was his first year diving, so every part of the process was new to him. He was a little intimated by the crowds and other divers. Even though he was nervous, he got through his first four dives very well. His scores were high. He was tied for first place. While getting ready for his last dive, someone said something that took his mind away, distracting him from concentrating on the dive. When his turn arrived, he missed it completely, landing on his back.
>
> After the meet, he came over to me in tears. He began to tell me about the meet.
>
> "Grandpa, it was horrible. After hitting the water, all tangled up, I climbed out of the water and everyone was

laughing at me. Even my coach was laughing. I can't ever go to another meet again," the boy exclaimed.

My first thought was to say, "Your coach wasn't laughing at you; neither was anyone else. This is no big deal. Suck it up; there will be other diving meets. In fact, you will have to learn to handle life's disappointments; this isn't a major one of them." But I didn't. Instead, I tried a recently learned listening technique.

Here is what I said: "It must have felt terrible for you to have that last dive go so badly, especially with all of the parents watching. When you came out of the swimming pool, seeing everyone staring at you must have made you uncomfortable. I am sure it didn't feel very good."

"Yes, Grandpa, that is how I felt." He looked at me and then exclaimed, "You understand!"

After the conversation, he was happy and went on his way with his second-place ribbon. What I learned was he didn't want a lecture, but instead, he wanted for me to know how he felt at the time of his mishap. He just wanted me to share his pained experience with him. The best result from this conversation is now my grandson feels his grandpa understands him. It has bettered our relationship.

To be a great listener, you have to put a tremendous amount of effort into it. Becoming a good listener takes a great detail of hard work. You have to see beyond the words, past the verbiage, and capture the nugget of true meaning. Meaning can get lost in connotations, missing the essence of the communication. *You may only be able to tell what you heard but not what was said.* The real message may have been missed. For this reason, it may be necessary to restate, rephrase, and repeat back for correct understanding of the message and its meaning, so what left the speaker's mind and heart will remain intact once it gets to you.

Grandpa G mentioned this story about two different meanings, which brought a smile to him, when talking to his grandson.

> My three-year-old grandson was proudly showing me how he put on his shoes by himself for our trip to the store. As I looked down, I noticed they were on the wrong feet—left shoe on the right foot and right shoe on the left foot.
>
> I told him, "grandson, your shoes are on the wrong feet."
>
> Pausing for a minute, then with raised eyebrow, he said, "Grandpa, don't tease me, theses are the only feet I got."

Few people know how to be an effective listener. Learning can be a difficult challenge for many people. But there is hope for us old guys—the specific skills of effective listening can be learned. It is our ultimate goal to integrate these skills into a progressive approach to hearing and understanding those around us.

Here is a story from a grandfather I thought was amusing, relating to the topic of listening at a deeper level.

> During one of our walks with my grandson, he asked me, "Grandpa, what causes arthritis?"
>
> Being a young teenager, and according to his mom, he was starting to decide if he wanted to begin experimenting with things teenagers do at his age (drugs, morality, drinking, etc.). His mom asked me to talk with him, encouraging him to not get involved with anything that could cause him harm. So with his question, I thought this would be a good teaching moment, and by using a backhanded approach, to get a point across to him.
>
> "I am not a 100 percent sure, but I understand it can be caused by drinking too much alcohol, doing drugs, lying to people, and problems with morality," I told him.

"Really, wow, that's not good," he muttered.

Feeling pretty smug in the way I expressed my point to him, I said, "By making good choices now, you won't have to worry about developing arthritis."

He responded, "Oh, I wasn't worried about me, I was just talking to Mom, and she said our minister at church just came down with a terrible case of arthritis."

Chapter 15

Stay In Tune

I find television very educating. Every time somebody turns on the set, I go into the other room and read a book.

—Groucho Marx

One of the saddest trends in our society today is the lack of communication among family members. From a survey in 1998, over a decade ago, the average couple only converses twenty-one minutes a week. With children, the amount of time was 5.4 minutes a day or 38 minutes a week. Yet the average time the TV was turned on exceeded seven hours per day (*AC Nielson Report*, 1998). When confronted with these numbers, back then most people were shocked and denied that it was possible; people especially said it was not true in their family. Today it is even worse, due to the invention of newer computers and smart phones. Now we see an even higher decline in time spent with families talking and doing things together. There is less time spent engaging in conversation with family members and joining in on family activities. Here are some of the latest results compiled by TV-Free America, from *AC Neilson Reports*.

Approximate number of studies examining TVs effects on children: 4,000

Number of minutes per week that parents spend in meaningful conversation with their children: 3.5

Number of minutes per week that the average child watches television: 1,680

Percentage of day care centers that use TV during a typical day: 70

Percentage of parents who would like to limit their children's TV watching: 73

Percentage of four- to six-year-olds who, when asked to choose between watching TV and spending time with their fathers, preferred television: 54

Hours per year the average American youth spends in school: 900 hours

Hours per year the average American youth watches television: 1,500

The same report indicated TVs are not on as long (6 hours, 47 minutes); however, the time not watching TV has been replaced by time spent on the computer and smart phones.

The Nielson Report of December 2012 came to the conclusion that the average person, regardless of age, sends close to four hundred texts per month. It is suggested the average teenager processes 3,417 texts a month—teenage girls with an average of 3,952, while the average teenage boy makes 2,815.

When I asked an eighteen-year-old grandson about this number—because I couldn't believe it!—he said, "Oh yeah, I often will go over four thousand per month."

"How do you know?" I asked.

Giving me a look expressing *Duh . . .* he responded, "I check at the end of the month on the phone for the total monthly texts."

The use of the Internet and electronics devices can become as addictive as a habit-forming drug. This is especially true with teenagers. All parts of our psychological makeup are affected like an addiction—dependence, behavior patterns, fear of loss, stress reactions, anxiousness, and obsessiveness.

According to a report on *CBS News* January 20, 2010, titled "Youth Spend 7+ Hours Daily Consuming Media," the average six-year-old and younger watch TV and other media for two hours per day, and children eight to eighteen years old spend seven hours daily consuming media. Overall, the time in noncommunications has risen at least one-third higher, because of the draw of the TV and the computer (including games, school assignments, research, searching the Web, conversation via texting, Facebook, Twitter, videos, etc.).

The first five years of life are considered a critical time for brain development when 85% of intellectual, personality and skills are accomplished in healthy children. It takes up to age twelve for the brain to become fully organized (*Wisconsin Council on Children & Family, Brain Development and Early Childhood*). TV and other electronic media can get in the way of exploring, playing, and interacting with parents and others, which encourages learning and healthy physical and social development.

As kids get older, too much screen time can interfere with activities such as being physically active, reading, doing homework, playing with friends, and spending time with family.

One grandfather told me something I thought was an interesting change from when our generation was in our teen years. He said two of his grandsons were turning sixteen and had no desire to learn how to drive. "Heck, we couldn't wait to drive. That was the ultimate independence for a teenager when we were young."

I asked him what he thought was the reason for their lack of desire.

He said he believed they had become too passive in their wants and needs. "They just want to play video games, watch TV, and hang out with friends. Their goals are undefined and wandering. I see them at home flop down in front of the TV or computer and stay there for hours. Letting it entertain them with little effort on their part," he said with dismay.

Children seem to be the group most affected by the decline of communication in the family. Over time, children have moved away from active outdoor games, lingual interaction, playing with toys, and family games requiring verbal communication. The currently preferred form of entertainment usually involves computer games, smart-phone activity or television watching. For parents, these forms of entertainment provide an electronic babysitter, allowing them to disengage and concentrate on their own activities. Families today are becoming more disassociated from each other than at any known time in history.

However, computers and TV in moderation can be a good thing. Preschoolers can get help learning the alphabet, languages, and simple math on computers or television. Older children can learn about wildlife on nature shows, find books, search for information in all categories, get the news and discover the background behind current events, and find help with homework.

Parents can keep up with current events on the evening news. Watching a favorite family show can be an excellent family activity. Computers, if used correctly, help with interfamilial communications and various other positive functions.

But despite its advantages, too much television can be detrimental:

- Children who consistently spend more than four hours per day watching TV are more likely to be overweight.
- Kids who view violent acts are more likely to show aggressive behavior but also fear that the world is scary and that something bad will happen to them.
- TV characters often depict risky behaviors, such as drinking, smoking, and participating in inappropriate physical situations, which may reinforce gender-role and racial stereotypes.

Children's advocates are divided when it comes to solutions. Although many urge for more hours per week of *educational* programming, others assert that *zero* TV is the best solution. And some say it's better for parents to control the use of TV and to teach children that it's for occasional entertainment, not for constant escapism.

Many children have a hard time distinguishing between reality and make-believe. The advancement in graphics, digital and computer-generated images have made it hard not to believe the pictures are, in fact, true. Children are becoming desensitized to horrible situations and moral standards. Death and pain are not real to young minds.

A few years ago, a church in Utah (Church of Jesus Christ of Latter-day Saints, also known as the Mormon Church), which was concerned with decay of family involvement caused by the effects of TV, decided to do a voluntary experiment with members of their congregation. They selected ten volunteer families to stop watching TV for three months. Only three families made it through the whole ninety days.

The successful families discovered during the test that each family member had become more interested in each other. One mother said, "The initial withdrawal was horrible for all of us. We had no idea how TV had weaved itself and become so intertwined in our daily lives. Our eyes were opened at several levels. We didn't realize how little we did communicate as individuals in the family before turning off the TV."

On the other hand, the other seven families mentioned reasons why it was so difficult to stay on course and why they failed. They described how each family member didn't want to sacrifice programs that had become a part of their lives, such as sports events, favorite shows, news, movies, cartoons, or just simply the routine of being passive and relaxing as the entertainment came to them.

One of the parents of a family who only lasted two weeks said, "It was too hard to find things to do as a family and as individuals. We liked coming home and turning on the TV and doing nothing. You have to work at entertaining yourself. Children would fight more and be more demanding of my time. It was just easier to turn on the TV."

As a society, we are addicted to TV, computers, and social media. I am concerned and maybe feel sorry for the next generation of children growing up in this environment of easy access to such passive entertainment. There is a fear that the art of verbal communications could be severely damaged or lost.

Now, Grandpa, don't just go in there and demand the children turn off their electronic devices. Here is what Grandpa G says,

> I have found if I just holler "Turn off the TV (or computer)!" the children are upset with me. They may be in the middle of a game or show, and I am creating an irritation with them. Half the time they are so heavily involved in the game, they don't even hear me talking to them. What I do instead is walk into the room where the child is watching TV or playing a game, and join in for a few minutes. And then, during a commercial break, or at a stopping point in the game, I will then have the child turn off the device. Going to the child conveys you're serious about your request; otherwise children interpret this as a mere preference.

I found one particular reference (Kiger, Patrick. July 2013. "It's a Fact: We Watch Too Much TV." AARP Magazine) pertaining to grandparents use of television and computers. It indicated the number-one usage of time by grandparents was either in front of the TV or on the computer—in excess of 50 percent of their time. They had the highest percentage of any group of all age levels of spending their valuable time, planted in front of a screen, as if they had grown roots to the floor in their favorite chairs. The following reasons—or excuses—were listed as the favorites for why grandparents spent so much time in front of electronic equipment:

- physical limitations, not being able to perform other active functions
- being too tired—it was "just easier"
- lack of ambition
- limited funds for other activities
- nothing else to do

- watching favorite shows
- communicating via computer
- keeping current on world events (news, politics, celebrities, religious activities)
- sports events
- computer writing activities (books, letters, e-mail, family pictures)
- viewing movies
- viewing documentaries
- viewing history programs
- passive entertainment

Grandpa, you might want to turn off the TV or computer and find ways to start talking to your family members.

Every year there used to be a National TV Turnoff Week. This meant shutting down the boob tube and turning your grandchildren on to . . . well, almost anything else.

The goal of TV Turnoff Week was simple: *Reduce the amount of time children spend in front of the television and on computers.* The event's organizers suggested several alternatives to the visual screen, and many community groups and libraries offered special after-school activities for children as alternatives to television or computer during the week.

While TV Turnoff Week was directed toward all ages, it was especially important for grandparents and adults to serve as role models by turning off the TV themselves. To be sure, trying it now will be a test of willpower.

Chapter 16

Steer Clear of Arguments

"Will you kids stop arguing?" "But, Grandpa, this is how we communicate."

Words spoken in anger will never be forgotten, by either the receiver or giver.

—Grandpa G

One of the grandpas told me of a research project he was involved with in the 1960s. It was at a research laboratory in California. The premise of the study was to teach chimpanzees how to drive. They had modified several small-engine cars for the experiment. After several weeks of teaching the mechanics of the car, they developed a course for the animals. The initial project was very promising. The chimps took to the concept with great ease.

Until we came to the major problem. The chimps were being taught the rules of the road. The problem that derailed the program was the simple signal light. The chimps were taught the three choices of the signal light: green for go, red for stop, but the yellow gave no clear action. As the chimps approached the signal light and the yellow appeared, there were only two courses of action by the chimps. One would brake and stop in the middle of the intersection and another would press the gas pedal and speed through. In both cases, it resulted in an accident. As the result of the accident, the chimp drivers would become very agitated at the handler or the other driver chimp.

Upon the conclusion, it was determined the behavior of the chimps came from black-and-white thinking. They made a decision, based upon their training, and it was final. They followed that training to the letter. When an accident occurred, they were upset, because they knew they were right. It appeared to them it shouldn't have happened, and it was somebody else's fault.

The reason for mentioning this study is to explain the difference and possible similarities between human beings and the chimp. Often a person establishes a pattern in his or her life, which will stay as a pattern forever even if there is better, clearer choice for making a decision—just like the chimpanzee. The reason is because of a feeling and belief that it is the right choice. A person will not change behavior or choice for the simple reason that it is the *right* or *correct* choice. In the mind, the right or correct selection exists; one is right and will not change even if there is a better option. To many of us, it is about being right, not about being effective.

The point is just being right is having a shortsighted view of what should be seen as a bigger picture. When dealing with grandchildren, spouses, or children, holding your ground because you're right can end up missing the mark of what is the most important goal for obtaining the best solution—that everyone is served.

Arguments are fed by people trying to prove they are right. Great solutions can be disregarded in the name of righteousness. Sometimes, it is wiser to be flexible, even if a person feels he is in the right.

Another cause for arguments sometimes comes from what starts as a playful discussion that might be labeled as *only teasing* and then turns into a heated battle with hurt and damaged feelings being the result. It can happen in an instant, the movement from conversation to argument is so quick and the response so passionate that those involved can lose sight of what happened and how it happened.

But if conflict does erupt and the differences between those involved in the argument are ignored, or not accepted, or resolved without mutual respect, then one or both parties may believe the result of the conflict discredits some precious, personal integrity. The perception of a slur on one's integrity is often experienced as a threat, and the position becomes personalized.

The worst-case scenario is easily demonstrated with the motorist displaying road rage. As one expressed, "The other guy was such an angry driver at my mistake, he let me know how he felt, insulting my honor, my family, my dog, and my ancestors clear back to Adam."

Subjects such as politics, religion, rules, relationships, dress styles, morality, work, culture, weather, military, experimentation, or anything that has two—or more—different point of views can spark a heated debate.

A grandfather told me of an argument he had with his grandson about religion. The grandfather had been in the same religion for many years; his parents were members of the same faith, and the boy's parents were members of the same faith. So when the teenager announced to Grandpa he was joining another religion, the reaction was quick and pointed.

"What do you mean you are going to join another church?" Grandpa exclaimed.

"I think their views are closer to what I believe," said the boy.

"Our family has always been members of _____ Church—it is your heritage. It is what you should do," Grandpa said.

"But that isn't how I feel about its beliefs," the boy explained.

"I don't care how you feel! It is about being right. And you are wrong to feel that way!" Grandpa expressed.

Arguments are often created because a person will take a superior attitude over another. This is true especially when regarding feelings.

Feelings are neither right nor wrong. Let me say that again: *feelings are neither right nor wrong.* They just exist.

We are all entitled to our own feelings. *They are ours.* Nobody has the right to tell a person how he or she should feel. Whenever a person takes the opinion he is right, and the other person should agree with his position, what he is actually expressing to them is that their feelings aren't acceptable, their thoughts are less-valued, or their feelings are not as important as his.

When one has a strong feeling or inclination it can be used to confirm emotions like disappointment, anger, sadness, happiness, hate, or fear. Instead of questioning the feelings, it is better to try to understand what the other person is feeling inside. Be a good listener, without judgment. Try to put yourself in the other's shoes to understand why someone might feel that way. Only after doing this will you be able to establish a deeper connection into your and your loved one's inner life. I am not saying you have to agree, but rather to have some empathy with what the other is experiencing. You are you, not the other, and will never fully comprehend how someone else is feeling inside, but you can be interested in trying.

When conversing with a grandchild particularly, before taking an opposing opinion, which can set you argument-bound, take the time to listen to the grandchild's point of view first. Try to pick up what he or she is feeling first, not just what he is saying. The reality is *feelings will always trump words.* If you do *hear* these feelings, you will be able to express how you feel as well, and in return your grandchild will be less reactive. This can establish a foundation to help prevent an argument.

Don't misunderstand, I am not saying to not argue. Arguments are actually a sign that you both want the best out of your relationship. If you never disagree, it can mean that one of you is just giving in repeatedly, which will damage the relationship over time every bit as much as fighting can. People are unique, and sometimes they don't see eye-to-eye on things. *Arguing* is actually a natural part of developing a strong bond with your grandchild. The closer you become, the more you get to know each other on a deeper level, and the more likely you will disagree. This is healthy. Especially if you encourage honest, friendly debate where everyone develops the ability to stand up for themselves.

Just stay within the following proper bounds:

- Stay calm, *nerves of steel.*
- Use language that is positive.
- Don't personally attack, appeal to higher values.
- Search for the best result, look for win-win solution.
- Don't let it get out of hand.
- Don't build a wall between, during, or afterward.
- Ask questions.
- Listen carefully, two ears, one mouth.
- Be prepared to concede a point.
- Smile, use humor—it will throw them off.
- Have respect.

Arguments are never won; the loser only concedes until the next battle.

Chapter 17

Tell Me a Story, Grandpa

Grandpa, can you please tell me a story? Please, please, please. . . .

Children of all ages love stories. They never get tired of a good story. Storytelling has been with mankind since the beginning of time. Good stories have been and will continue to be passed on for years. Stories are the lifeblood of society. In every culture, the story is the centerpiece of communication. From the caveman to ancient civilizations to Native Americans to pioneers, even to today's modern families, people have gathered around fire circles and family dwellings to share experiences and stories.

Telling a story is the conveying of events in images, words, and sounds, often by improvisation or embellishment. Stories or narratives have been shared in every culture as a means of entertainment, education, folklore, preservation of traditions, and to teach moral values.

Stories are universal in that they can leap across obstacles, whether it be language, cultural, or age. Storytelling can be used as a teaching and learning tool for developing values, social graces, ethics, and acceptability. Learning is most effective when it takes place in social surroundings of familiar groups of people—family, religious, and community—where information is shared. Stories provide a method to relate knowledge in an approved context. All men desire knowledge, excitement, emotion, and entertainment.

Our understanding of our ancestors as well as our knowledge of humanity are based on stories that we embrace in our memories, so we can recall and share them again. Our lives are engulfed in stories. We are a storytelling species, both as individuals and as groups, fascinated with tales of great feats and great failures. We share experiences from our own lives and those of others by telling them as stories. Our thoughts are best remembered in stories. We think in stories. We relate in stories. We communicate in stories. Stories help us remember events, teachings, facts, and duties. We know a human mind will remember better when a presentation is attached to a story. All great presenters use stories as the basis of their presentation. Facts can be very dry and boring, but if inserted into a story it not only captures the essence of the point, it can appeal to analytical thinking.

Effective education is brought about through stories, because listeners become engaged and better able to comprehend and remember. While the story is being shared, listeners are involved; they are able to imagine new perspectives, explore new ideas, and be motivated to try something different. A storyteller can create lasting personal connections, inspire better problem-solving, and promote better comprehension of life's problems. The storyteller will often gain more than the listener. A storyteller and a listener can participate in the experience together. Both grow from the story.

Storytellers have shaped our societies and the way we think for all of recorded history. I imagine the first people would gather in groups to tell of their day's experience with their people each day. The first recorded drawings on cave walls suggest a deep emotional need to share life's adventures. Humankind is born with a driving desire to pass on the lessons learned, from important matters to just plain everyday events.

With storytelling, came the birth of distinct individual heroes, kings, gods, villains, and magicians. Religions were formed. Great deeds in battle, with heroes strengthened by the gods, and terrible defeats, punished in equal measure, were portrayed.

Community pride, character development, and social bonding emerged. The roots of all teaching, communication, human connection, and religion all lie within stories.

All ancient languages contained stories of deeds done by kings or heroes. Many stories were passed down for centuries orally before they were committed to literature. Some of the great Shakespearean plays were probably influenced by ancient Greek tragedies. Major events, ancient magic, legends, and teaching stories (myths) were eventually transcribed from oral form to writings. Imagination was intertwined to create even higher levels of fable and beliefs.

Like the movies of today, all stories had a hero (representing good), a villain (representing evil), a moral dilemma, and the success of making good choices to prove good will triumph over evil. This taught the audience that godly standards were better than ungodly actions. Thus, it created acceptable standards of living one's life in society.

Modern plays and theater developed in Western civilization as a method for retelling the classic stories and cultivating religious and political views. Folklore, tall tales, and plays presented to those who couldn't read or write provided a method of understanding for the general population. Many of the common stories told by the fireplace, then as now, were presented by grandfathers, grandmothers, and elder storytellers.

But why is this important to you as a grandfather?

Because children crave stories, and they will spontaneously make them up if they can't receive them any other way. On the other hand, classic storytelling is becoming a lost art. Personal stories of heritage, ancestry, and recent family are forfeited with the death of each person of each generation, voices silenced, never to be heard again. It is sad that the wealth of knowledge gained throughout a person's lifetime is erased, blotted out, and permanently removed with no further access to important details concerning family members or historical data, all because of death. Statistical reports, limited writings, and hearsay don't tell the true story. Each rising generation wants to know where they came from.

Whom do they ask? People are so busy living their own lives, they don't take—or have—the time to seize the opportunity to acquire information through the eyes of the previous generation. This is especially true of parents, trying to survive in today's world. You often hear, "I will write that down someday; it is on my to-do list . . . as soon as I have the time." Or they rationalize to themselves by saying, on some future date, "I will get to it. I know I need to do it." The sad truth is getting to the information never seems to happen . . . until it is too late. This is not because they don't have a true desire or real intention; they just run out of time.

Some of the most common responses of the survey dealt with respondents' regret for not capturing more details about their own grandfathers' lives.

They made statements like the following in response to questions about what they wished they had asked their grandfather while he was still alive. Even though I did not specifically ask a question about what if they had a second chance to talk to their grandfather, these responses came out in our conversations.

> I wished I had asked more about his childhood.
> I wished he would have told me about being a cowboy when he was young.
> His experiences in the military.
> How did he meet Grandma?
> What were some of the hardships they went through?
> What was the funniest thing that happened to him?
> Did he have a favorite pet?
> Tell me about his parents?
> Did he have any scary stories?
> What were my parents like when they young?
> Did he have any adventures?
> Did he ever get into trouble?

The list went on and on, people searching for lost answers.

For those who lost the opportunity to glean information from their parents and grandparents, there is no hope. But grandfathers of today, you do have the good fortune to still share stories about your lives with your grandchildren. They do have the time. *I personally believe, back to ancient times, that most stories were told by the elders so traditions and history would not be lost.*

Today, most of the industrialized world is peopled by literary cultures. Stories are mostly recounted in books, movies, filmed documentaries, and online. You find oral stories commonly told today only at home, which is the traditional root of stories, or at special festivals and a few other events.

Sadly, with the rise of technological storytelling devices, the cultural prominence of storytelling as an art form is transforming. Traditional storytelling is dying out, replaced by video, the Internet, mass-market books, radio, and other forms of new media. You can still experience oral storytelling at storytelling festivals, and there are many organizations throughout the United States, Canada, and Europe that promote storytelling and help to train new storytellers, but few people can make a living at it.

Storytelling *per se*, however, will never die out. Mothers and fathers will always tell bedtime stories to their children, and stories will always be an important part of our culture. But much of the traditional place of stories has been taken over by Hollywood; the same thing may be happening in India, China, and other parts of the world where mass media is gradually becoming the normal form of transmission of culture.

Oral presentation is being lost to visual stimulation. Little minds don't have to employ imagination, fill in the gaps, use their minds to expand the seeds of thought and wonder as words take them only partway, allowing them to insert their own images and conclusions for the full experience of the story.

One night while I was visiting with my grandchildren, my daughter began to read a book of stories from one of our ancestors to them. It was a book of adventures of a young girl. As the story unfolded with challenges and funny situations, my grandchildren became deeply involved, as if they were living the adventure along with the story's heroine. Each child added his or her own interpretation to the storyline as it moved along. Their faces were immersed in thought and wonder. Each laughed at the appropriate places, showing fear on cue where it seemed necessary. I remember thinking *How could a simple little book bring so much pleasure to children?* After the book was finished, the adventures lingered on in their minds and conversations. What tragedy it would have been if someone hadn't written down the stories of her childhood!

The question is how much will we lose when traditional storytelling gives way completely to modern media? And how much of a family's moral standards will be replaced by Hollywood's interpretation of acceptable lifestyles? It has yet to be answered.

Yet, if used properly, the Internet may be able to preserve much of the individuality of the oral story, even if the spontaneity, facial expressions, voice inflections, and the gradual changing of the story, which has always been part of the art form, may be lost.

The question becomes, how do you tell an awesome story which creates a lasting memory?

What I found when talking to grandfathers many don't know how to tell a good story, which causes them to never venture or divulge their experiences. This is true with the following example.

While in discussion with one grandfather, he mentioned, "I am not very good at telling stories. I have a hard time remembering some of the details. I don't feel my stories are very interesting. So I just don't tell any. When a grandchild asks me to tell a story, my mind goes blank."

I asked him, "Could you tell me a story about when you were young?"

He proceeded with what he thought was a story: "I played football, on the varsity team in high school, it was hard. We were good. I played linebacker. I liked playing for my school. In our final game, I scored."

What? He was right; he was very boring. When telling a story, you have to make it exciting, motivating, and interesting. I started looking at the story, thinking there must be more. Inside, I felt it had the makings of a great story . . . with a good storyline and the right kind of details, it could be a fantastic story! I proceeded to ask more questions and found some wonderful details, originally omitted by this Grandpa.

Let's look at the same story told by Grandpa G, but with using storytelling techniques I will discuss after the story. Now, Grandpa G did glean the full information from the original grandpa which the original grandpa had failed to present in his story.

Grandpa G began . . .

> When I was a teenager, I was lucky enough to go to the best high school in the state, East High, home of the Mustangs. Its football team was ranked number one in the state and one of the best in the entire country. The team always finished first, second, or third in the state. Growing up, I used to dream of one day playing on the East High football team.
>
> When I told one of my friends while we were in middle school that I was going try out for the football team, he looked at me laughing and said, "You are too small."
>
> It was true I was smaller than most of boys my age. However, ever since I was little, my dad told me if I worked hard enough, I could do anything . . . if I believed I could. I knew if I had any chance of making the team, I would have to put in the time and pour everything I had into becoming faster and stronger. It became my passion.
>
> Each day, I would be on the field running, back and forth, end to end, side to side, just as fast as I could, full-speed always, until I couldn't run another step. Every inch of my entire body would ache after each workout. I would be so exhausted. But I knew I couldn't stop after the field workouts, for it was only half of becoming

stronger. For the second half of the program, I would head for the gym to lift weights—to strengthen my muscles and endurance. For hours, days, weeks, even months, I worked very hard following this routine. Many times, I wanted to give up and quit, but I didn't, because I had a goal to accomplish constantly pushing me.

Then one day, I looked in the mirror after my workout to realize my muscles were twice their original size. I already knew my speed had doubled, and I was becoming faster and faster. It felt so good and gave me renewed energy, but most of all, it gave me pleasure in my achievement. This inspired me to work even harder.

Yet, still knowing I remained shorter than most of the other players, I didn't know if I would make the varsity squad, let alone be on the starting team. I went to every practice and gave everything I had to prove I was good enough to play on the varsity team.

Finally, in my last year of high school, my strength and speed paid off. No linebacker was quicker or stronger. Every day I played as hard as I could, constantly working to prove to myself and the coaches that I was the best linebacker on the defense. I not only made the team, but I made more tackles than any other member on the team. The coaches would continually give me compliments about my performance on and off the field. It felt good to finally achieve something I worked so hard for, and it was the highlight of my life.

In my last game in high school, we were playing against the number-one-rated Panthers for the state championship. I was extremely nervous. You could feel the tension everywhere—in the stands, with the players on the sidelines, and even in the excitement of the announcer's voice. The whole state was watching the game on TV. The stadium was filled to capacity, forty thousand plus in the stands, watching us. This was promoted as the Battle of the Undefeated, for neither the Mustangs nor the Panthers had lost a game.

It was a hard-fought, close game. Neither team was showing any weakness. Whoever won this game would have to earn it. Both teams had scored twenty-one points, and we were tied with the final seconds ticking away.

The other team had the ball on the thirty-fifth yard line with ten seconds to go on the clock. They were too far to make an attempt at a field goal, so we knew they would either have to do a running play or a pass. This would be the final play of the game. As they were coming to the line, I looked over at the other linebacker, Chuck, my good friend and fellow team member.

I loved Chuck, he was so funny. Throughout the season, whenever he would make a tackle and while the other player was on the ground, he would ask the player he tackled a question just to play with his mind.

Questions such as, "Do you know why Jefferson was a better president than Lincoln?"

"Do you know why you should start your running with your left foot instead of your right?"

"Do you know why God made you?"

"Do you know why you shouldn't eat turnips?"

Each game had a new question. After being tackled four or five times, the person would start to try to answer, but Chuck would be gone before they could answer, leaving them frustrated. All Chuck wanted to do was to get them thinking about something other than the game. It was so funny to watch players on the other side—they'd be pointing at Chuck, talking about him. I can only imagine what they said.

Chuck's question for this game was, "Do you know why the Mustangs are better than the Panthers?" He talked me into doing the same thing in this last game. On every tackle, I would ask the downed player, "Do you know why the Mustangs are better than the Panthers?" They would give me the strangest look.

So here we were. I caught his eye, and he returned my look. We both knew this was the last play before end of the season and probably of our football careers. We both felt they were going to pass the ball. So I signaled for us both to rush the passer at the same time.

He agreed and replied, "I will go in low, and you go in high."

The ball was hiked to the quarterback. We both charged as fast as we could. The quarterback saw me and started to move away from me. Just then Chuck hit him full-force, smacking the ball with his hand. The ball flew up in the air. As I watched it sail up, it seemed to be in slow motion, suspended in time, right above my head. I reached up and caught it on the run.

For sixty-five yards, I ran as fast as I could, all those days of running had made me fast . . . and strong—nobody could catch me. The gun went off as I passed the five-yard line, and I scored the winning touchdown. That day, I stood taller than any linebacker in school history.

Chuck came running up to me in the end zone and whispered, "Do you know why the Mustangs are better than the Panthers?" Then he smiled and said, "Because the Mustangs just won the state championship!"

Before I get into the techniques Grandpa G used, I want to explain some of the tendencies I have discovered about men. Unfortunately, I have found too many men don't spend enough time in the details of their life. They seem more interested in the bigger picture. Their minds look at the broad strokes. This often ends up with results of communicating quickly and in as few words as possible to convey a simple message. For instance, how men greet each other is totally different from women. A man's greeting may consist of a nod, a wave, or saying something like "Hey, how are you doing?" or "How's it going?" With this type of greeting, there is no intention of receiving a response other than "Okay, doing well," or just "well." They are through with their communication. No follow-up questions or deeper interaction is necessary.

Meanwhile, women greet one another with comments such as, "How are you feeling?" and then proceed to ask for details about family, work, church, friends, shopping, health, home, and styles. Women use more words to discuss their interactions with those around them.

A friend of mine once counted as an experiment the number of words used by women versus men in normal conversation. The results found women use four to ten times more words than men in the same time period. In most situations, men took a direct approach, zeroing in on the point they wanted to convey, while women shared more detail, gathered more information, and took their time before getting to the point. Women seemed to enjoy the process of conversation, while men enjoyed getting to the end with the desired intent accomplished. This means most men need to work with details and expansion of words to create a more vivid story.

Thinking about this, I decided to talk to my friend Grandpa G. He is considered one of the greatest storytellers of all time. He came from a long line of storytellers. His great-uncle William was legendary in his day. Grandpa G had grown up listening to his uncle's stories. Whenever Uncle William would come to visit, the whole family would gather in excited anticipation to hear him tell of his new adventures as well as retelling many of the old family favorites. It was a training ground for Grandpa G.

Grandpa G once told me he didn't see himself as a good storyteller when he was younger, so he decided to ask Uncle William if he would give him some pointers that would make him a better presenter of stories. His uncle was thrilled to share some of his techniques. Grandpa G wrote them down, and from then on, he would incorporate them into all of his stories. Now he is considered a master storyteller. When I asked Grandpa G, he said I could share them with you.

Grandpa G's Notes from Uncle William

The audience has a very important role in storytelling—for their minds are the canvas on which the teller paints his tale. Remember how a few years ago, the great radio programs were done only through the airways? The actors would create suspenseful stories full of adventures, only using voice and sounds. For those of us who were young, our imaginations would fill in the details, making the story our own. There was no need of visual pictures, for we captured it in our minds (*The Shadow,* my favorite program every Sunday night: "Who knows what evil lurks in the hearts of men? *The Shadow knows!*"). The descriptions were detailed but not too detailed, for they gave us the opportunity to use our own experiences and thoughts to envision the particulars. Think in terms of your audience only hearing you over the radio. How would that change your choice of words and voice presentation?

There is a big advantage to being in front of your audience. Oral storytelling involves much interaction between teller and listener. You get to keep listeners absorbed in the story by playing to their emotions and the constant changing of reactions. It is like a game of chess, trying to stay ahead of the other player—in this scenario, the other players are the listeners. It isn't as easy these days, for I have observed that our audiences have lost some of the skills to follow a narrated story and see things in their minds. They have gotten lazy, because of the technology of videos and computers providing so much detail for them. Storytelling has become more difficult. Attention spans are shorter and more demanding, more sophisticated, yet less able to independently imagine or visualize. People seem to need more visual stimulation.

Once you settle on a story, you will want to spend plenty of time with it. It will take a considerable period of time and a number of tellings (at least fifty times) before a story becomes your own. Read it over and over, absorbing the meaning of what you want to convey. *Analyze it for its appeal,* the word pictures you want your listeners to see, and the mood you wish to create. *See it, visualize it!* Imagine sounds, tastes, scents, colors. Only when you see the story vividly yourself can you make your audience see it! *Live with your story,* make it a part of you until the characters and setting become as real to you as people and places you know. Check for its cultural value, research other specific interpretations.

When developing your story, try to use the following suggestions to make the story come alive and captivating.

- Tell stories that you love. Your own excitement will come out in the story.
- Make the story relate to the group as close as possible. If they can associate with the story, then they will be more engaged.
- Try to keep the story as brief and simple as possible (especially for younger children)—keep to the heart of the story.
- Don't get lost in unrelated or uninteresting details.
- Set the stage about what, why, where, and how it is going to happen or has happened. Describe the characters and settings, and help them sympathize with the character's feelings.
- Establish conflict: man against himself, man against others, man against nature. This includes team against team, evil against good. Conflict creates excitement.
- Use foreshadowing: hinting of things to come builds suspense, allows the crowd to guess ahead, creates more involvement. *What is going to happen?*
- Stimulate the senses so listeners feel, smell, touch, and see vivid pictures. This helps their minds capture the fullness of the story.
- Use dialogue, people talking back and forth. It spices up the interactions between the characters.
- Insert humor: humor makes it fun. Laugher is like jam on toast; it makes the story sweet and appealing.
- Tell stories that touch your heart. The stories people remember the most are ones that touch their heart.
- Aim your story at the youngest ones in the room. After all, all ages are young at heart, and it makes the story easy to understand. Plus, it keeps the little ones interested and absorbed in the story.
- Pace your story; don't rush through it. Take your time, put in pauses for dramatic effect. Let the information sink in, getting soaked up into imagination. Vary

speeds, use tone inflections, be animated with facial expressions and gestures, body movement.

If you review the difference between how Grandpa G told the story and how the original grandpa presented it you can see the techniques.

This was a real story, it happened, as told to me by the grandfather who experienced it. The original grandpa didn't make the story come alive; he just listed the basic facts. In contrast, Grandpa G added all of the elements to make a great story: It was a story he loved. He set the stage. The audience could relate to it. He gave it foreshadowing, hinted at what was going to happen. He used dialogue with characters' personalities. There was some humor. The story touched your heart. Last, it didn't get caught up in too many details.

If you learn how to apply these elements in every story, it comes alive. The story will be remembered and ingrained in your audience's minds. They will feel the story and love it. During the process of telling the story, you will connect to your listeners and they to you. Finally, you will be highly regarded as a great storyteller!

Grandpa G told me there is another technique you can employ while telling a story if you want to bring in—or engage—the group of listeners. This method, if interjected correctly, can also reveal a personal attachment to the story. You can accomplish this by asking a question or making a statement in the middle of a story. For example:

- Have you ever felt that way?
- Does that make sense to you?
- What do you believe he was thinking?
- Do you think he was doing the right thing?
- Could you do that?
- How do you think he felt at that moment?
- Wow, can you imagine?
- Would that scare you?

Or leading statements like these:

- Listen to the next part; it is funny . . .
- I like this, because . . .
- Remember this part, because later . . .
- I think I would be frightened.
- That would make me feel so proud.

Grandpa G says he often uses one additional way of expanding the story—using familiar comparisons or parables. This method allows the audience to clearly see, feel, and experience the effects of the story's elements. It lets them mentally relate through association, by taking them into a familiar setting with a commonly known story or activity we all can relate to. For example:

- He struggled like a chicken breaking free of its shell . . .
- It is the same red as an apple.
- It was colder than being locked in a freezer for an hour . . .
- His smile was so big, a mortician couldn't have removed it . . .
- It stunk so bad that even flies wouldn't go near it . . .
- It felt like a thousand needles stabbing all at once . . .
- The effect was the same as the boy who falsely cried wolf . . .

In summation, I learned from Grandpa G that to be a great storyteller, it takes practice. For years, I have told stories, but not at the level I could have told them. So I began writing them down, adding the above elements, reciting them over and over, constantly fine-tuning them. I even recorded them to hear how they sounded to me.

(Note: Comedians will often take a voice recorder to their performances, recording the reactions of the audience to their jokes. Then they will add or take away material, depending on the reactions. They are always trying to prefect the material. It works.)

Slowly, my stories began to develop into wonderful stories, full of life and appeal. Now they are rewarding to both me and my listeners.

Chapter 18

Rambling Is the Death of a Story

I love this story.

A grandpa, while talking to his young grandson, got into one of his long-winded conversations with details dragging on and on, making it uninteresting to his grandson:

"In the old days, you had to know the ringtone of the phone—like for example, two short or two long rings—the phone line was shared by neighbors, allowing a person to listen to a neighbors' conversation . . . AT&T owned everything. Then Congress took them to court—"

The grandson, listening nervously, interrupted, "Grandpa, I think the dog has to go outside."

Grandpa said, "Okay, I guess you'd better take him outside."

The grandson took the dog through the door and said to the dog outside, "When Grandpa gets started, you have to have an exit strategy."

Grandpa, don't get caught up in the wilderness of yesteryears.

One item often mentioned in the surveys was how Grandpa would ramble on about things the listener knew nothing about. Your memories are just that, *your memories.* Sharing everything you know or everything you experienced is not interesting. Those listening start to become glassy-eyed, looking for an exit. It is an uncomfortable situation for the listener; he doesn't want to offend or hurt the feelings of the rambler, but at the same time, he has no interest in the information spilling out. It can be a similar feeling of panic as when the toilet bowl is about to overflow—you can't stop it; the water just keeps coming.

Often, it is hard for some grandpas to know what is an acceptable line for sharing stories, memories, and information—when it is too much, too boring, or too unrelated.

There is a perfect example of this when I was traveling with my parents as a young boy in the farming community of northern Arkansas, looking for my mom's cousin's home. We were deep in back country where there were no maps, and we were lost. This was before GPS systems, so your only hope was to find a friendly neighbor to give you directions. In those days, as you drove down a country road, everyone waved and said howdy. As we came to a split in the road, my dad wasn't sure which way to go. While we were stopped, pondering which way to go, an elderly gentleman happened to walk by. My dad stopped him to ask for directions.

"Do you know how to get to May Rearton's home?"

The old man paused as if he were gathering his thoughts; then in his thick, slow Arkansas drawl, he said, "May Rearton . . . isn't she one of those Swathford girls? You know the family that used to live over on Hycorn Creek with the eight girls? They had that big hound dog, which chased down Johnny Anderson by mistake and treed him like a raccoon—he was running through the edge of town screaming like a fool with that old dog, who mistook him for somebody else, biting at his heels. Johnny stayed in that tree screaming most of the day until one those girls came and got the dog. We all got a chuckle that day. For years, Johnny never went anywhere without looking to see if the hound dog was around."

He continued, "Wait. May wasn't a Swathford; I was thinking of Marylou. She married Tommy Trenton. They built the house over by Crooked Creek. You know, where Raiders Island used to be until the flood of '54 washed it away. Raider Island got its name because our boys used it during the war, and those dumb Yankees couldn't find them. It was a secret base, where they would hide and plan their next battle."

Continuing, he said, "No, it couldn't have been Tommy and Marylou; they lost that house when lightning hit that big Liberty Oak Tree. We called it Liberty Oak Tree because it had all the names of the raiders carved on it. That old tree fell down across their home, burning it to the ground. Some of my relatives had their names on that tree."

My dad looked at my mom with a look of help in his eyes. She yelled from the car, "May's last name was Green!"

The old boy asked, "Was she Perry and Betty Green's daughter? You know, the Greens weren't liked for many years around here. Her great-grandfather fought for the Union. He was a preacher, I believe. They had to move to Crane, Missouri, during the war for their own protection. They didn't believe in slavery like the rest of us. For a while, the folks around here felt they had turned on their neighbors and some kinfolk. After the war, they returned to find their home and property burnt down. But since then, all was forgiven, and their children have become a great part of our community."

He continued, "May married Percy Rearton. He was named after his uncle Percy. His uncle Percy traveled all over the country, selling various household items. He was quite the fellow. Did you know he could shoot a squirrel from over two hundred yards away? I have seen him do it. We were in the woods behind the Hutchins's farm on Red Tail Mountain. It got its name because of the red tail fox—"

Dad interrupted, "Which is the best way to get to Percy and May's home?"

The old gentleman said, "Well, if you go to the left, you will pass where the old flour mill used to be; then turn left again, it will take you by the Johnsons—nice folks, did you know their daughter, moved to New York City and became a high-priced lawyer? They don't see her very often . . ."

He then proceeded to tell about all of the families, one by one, their problems, successes, and history along that dirt road. All the time, my mom and two brothers and I were sitting in the car on that hot and muggy Arkansas day. My dad kept trying to bring him back to find where Percy and May's home was located, but he would again wander off on another bit of information unrelated to directions.

After he told us about all the families who lived on the road if we turned left, he said, "But you don't want to turn left, because Percy brought some land off the road to the right."

What? All of us just threw up our hands in disbelief.

Then he started to share with us about all the families who ever lived on the road to the right.

Dad finally interrupted him again and said, "Thank you."

Then we drove off, turning to the right. We found cousin May's house. This was a true story. I believe if my dad hadn't cut him off, we would still be there today, listening to all the gossip from that old gentleman. Again, this illustrates the importance of staying on track and not rambling on about all your knowledge. Through the years, we have reflected on the experience as a funny occurrence to be retold at many family gatherings, but at the time it was frustrating.

One grandpa told me how he came to a personal conclusion when talking to his son and daughter-in-law while visiting the hometown of his youth. As they would drive by places, it would jog his memory and he would relate some activity that took place there.

"I would get excited telling these stories, one after another, as memories so precious to me would come to mind. What I didn't realize was these stories had no impact on my son and daughter-in-law. It wasn't that they didn't care; they just couldn't relate to the stories on a personal basis. What was meaningful to me didn't make the same impression on them. There was no connection to the times, the history, the atmosphere of the day, the humor, or the people. My children lived in a different world from the one I came from. I guess this is why each generation feels more comfortable talking to friends their own age who understand similar backgrounds and times. After some time, I saw the fatigued look in their eyes. It then dawned on me I had shared more than I should have shared."

One of the biggest truths grandpas need to remember when telling stories is that *this is your past, not theirs. Some things need to be left unsaid.*

An additional principle required when telling historical experiences, be sure of your facts. It is okay to put a *little blarney* in the story to make it more interesting, but be sure to keep to the true, basic storyline.

One grandpa was relating his experiences while in World War II. He even wrote a book about a certain battle in Europe in which he was involved.

He told me,

> I had related the story of the battle so many times, I felt I was an expert on the historical details of the battle. When someone suggested I write a book about the battle, I jumped at the chance. It was a big success. I would quote stories from the book to my grandchildren as I remembered them. I was so proud of my work. Then one day, someone found a lost documentary film talking about the battle, which was the same as in my book. Everyone had thought it and other details of the battle had been destroyed. I was invited to watch it as they unveiled it for the first time.

> I was horrified. It revealed a totally different story than the one I had written in my book. As the film was playing, I realized it was true and my remembered facts had gotten distorted over time. I had added little changes to make it more appealing on each telling of the story, until it didn't contain the real facts anymore. Yet, in my mind, I didn't comprehend or notice the small changes, which had led me so far astray from the original truth. The book I was so proud of, which I had shared with my children and grandchildren, was full of falsehoods.

> But more importantly, if historians use my book years from now as a resource of the battle, it will not be of the true story and the real facts will be lost. I feel bad and helpless, thinking of this.

When listening to him, I felt his pain and remorse for writing about a historical event and basically adding false information, which can never be removed. It would be like telling a Bible story such as Adam and Eve and having Adam eating the fruit first instead of Eve or maybe a story of the Old West like Custer's Last Stand and having him win, killing all the Native Americans (Indians).

Telling a great historical story means you have to stick to the basic truth, so your listeners can relate to the familiar story. Especially if they already know the story. When one strays away from original scripts, people have a tendency to not like it, because they remember how it is supposed to go. This is why some stories never get old, even when they are repeated many times.

Some readers will read the same book over and over, simply because they enjoy the story. It is just like watching the same old movie several times. This attitude also applies to any familiar, historical story. It doesn't matter if the people hear it for the first time or hundredth time, it will be enjoyed by its listening audience.

The story becomes like a trusted friend. Even though a person has heard the identical story quite a few times, he still enjoys hearing it again. He knows the plot. He knows the twists and turns. He has become part of the story. An interesting thing emerges when people hear a familiar story: a feeling is created. Because the audience knows what is about to happen, they think they have the inside track. They feel they own this knowledge. They feel special, like knowing the truth about Santa Claus while the rest of the family doesn't. Having prior knowledge of the story empowers them.

It is critical to know your story well, but be careful not to change from the common historical facts and truths.

Chapter 19

If It Is Private, Keep It Private

I can't believe you said that. What were you thinking?
—Wife to Husband

A child's mind is like a cloth which had bleach spilled on it. Once there, the permanent stains can never be removed.

A typical mistake made by storytellers is using information that is private or embarrassing to another individual. What some people think is funny is not to the person who experienced it. Sometimes it is so easy to get caught up in the story, we don't think about the consequences that might result from the details being revealed. Nobody wants his dirty laundry displayed before the world, especially to family and friends. It is inappropriate to share private information to the world. If you are going to use a particular story about a family member or a friend *get their permission first!* Otherwise, you may create a rift in the family or lose a friend. Remember, personal is personal and public is public, so don't mix the two. Stories shouldn't be gossip or hearsay about anyone. The same applies to individual and family secrets, especially when talking to children. (Secret means secret, not public.) That isn't entertaining, but often, it is just mean. Think before you talk.

As Grandpa G says, "Before I mention a story, I think of two things. First, will it hurt a person's feelings? Second, would I like it if the story were told about me?"

An example of this comes from a grandfather who was relating the time when he told a story that caused a major family division that still remains today.

> I was at a family function where we were all sharing the typical stories you do with each other in the family. When I decided to mention how my wife could get so uncontrollably mad about things and would brood over a matter, being totally absorbed in it. Like the time her sisters Jane and Addie took all her mother's handmade, beautiful quilts after she died, before any of the other siblings got any.
>
> Boy, was that the wrong thing to say. The reaction was immediate and deep. First, I insulted my wife, about her personal emotions, handling anger—she didn't talk to me for a month (she was so mad at me). Second, I started a family feud, because many of the family members didn't know that Addie and Jane took the quilts. It turned into a major battle between siblings and their families. All of this was created because of me saying something stupid. I am considered the bad guy in our family now. I sure wish I could go back and change that day.

Once words leave your mouth, they can't be unsaid. For good or evil, they are gone with no return ticket. This grandfather will forever be tarnished by his moment of using unthinking words.

This doesn't mean every story is off-limits. Many times, incidents that weren't funny at the time, told later are not only very appropriate but received with humor by everyone, including the person to whom it pertained.

Grandpa G told me this one.

> When we were first married, we bought a new Ford
> Galaxy, with the black vinyl top. My sweet young wife
> decided she would surprise me by washing the car
> while I was at work. Since we had to park our car near
> a tree, it often would have tree sap and bird droppings
> on the top. She thought it would be a good idea to give it
> a good, complete cleaning. Not knowing anything about
> vinyl, but a lot about household cleaning chemicals, she
> decided to use a bleach-based product. By the time I got
> home, the vinyl had not only cracked in thousands of
> pieces, it was peeling up and coming off, showing rusted
> metal underneath.
>
> It was a disaster. Our new car was in shambles. I
> found my wife inside with puffy, red eyes. She had been
> crying for hours. Knowing the next few words coming out
> of my mouth could determine the course of our marriage,
> I stopped for a moment and then put my arms around
> her and told her it was all right, besides we would now be
> able to easily find our car in a busy parking lot.
>
> Once her fear of me being mad was gone, she
> expressed her deep sorrow and regret to me. Whenever
> we went somewhere, people would ask us what happened
> to the car. Each time, she would look at me with terror
> in her eyes, afraid I would embarrass her in front of our
> friends and family. I never did. I would just say it was
> defective. Years later, I asked her if I could tell of the
> incident. She said yes, and now it is told with humor and
> delight for all of us.

There are so many things I like about this story. *First,*
Grandpa G could have gotten mad and belittled his wife,
possibly hurting their relationship in the long run, but he
didn't. *Second,* he could have embarrassed her in front of those
close to her, hurting her feelings and exposing raw emotions,
again he chose not to. *Third,* he asked her permission before
he shared the story with others. Sometimes, we all just repeat

stories without thinking of their impact on those involved, in the name of humor.

One last thought about storytelling: be careful when telling grandchildren about their own parents, your children. Don't be a tattletale, sharing their weaknesses, faults, problems, or failures with their children. *Build up* your children in front of your grandchildren. Your children are their parents, in whom they want to feel a sense of pride. It is hard enough being a parent without distractions from grandparents.

Grandpa G gave me some advice on this when I asked how he handled questions from grandchildren about their parents.

"Always be wise when questions arise from grandchildren concerning their parents. The secret is understanding the reason behind the question. If the question is negative in nature, answer positively. If the question is positive, you still answer positively. You always want to positively promote your children in the eyes of their children, who are your grandchildren," he said.

Here is an example he gave me:

> One time my eleven-year-old grandson asked if his dad was a hard child to raise. (Actually, my son did have his moments when there were some harsh confrontations.) At the time my grandson asked the question, his dad was standing right by me. He had a little look on his face, questioning what I was going to say.
>
> Here is how I responded: "Your dad was easy to raise. He did what he was told to do. He was almost perfect."
>
> My son, his dad, catching the cue, raised his arms high in the air looking at his son and said, "See, I told you I was a perfect child."
>
> It isn't whether my son was good or bad, but at that moment, he was elevated in front of his son. The grandchild saw his dad as being good. Every child longs to be proud of their parents. Their parents are often their heroes. Don't diminish their standing or status by saying something negative about your children.

Every grandpa needs to be able to tell stories to their grandchildren. So start today and begin your journey as the best storyteller ever to your grandchildren. Practice, *practice*, and *practice*. Learn and apply the techniques mentioned previously. Write down the stories. Stay to the important details of the story and don't ramble. Don't get lost in the wilderness of yesteryear. Keep from hurting people's feelings by using inappropriate or private, personal information. Most of all, relax and enjoy talking to your grandchildren.

Chapter 20

You're Still a Dad

Think of your child as your apprentice in life. Training never ends, no matter the age.

—Grandpa G

A child may grow too big for my lap, but never too big for my heart. Never lose the joy of being a parent. It is a privilege. Sometimes we forget the gift, caught up in the daily activities of life. The most important, the heaviest, and most weighted success will be cherished memories created with loved ones.

There is wonder as to why some people allow worldly anchors to come between the abundant joys of family activity, especially within the walls of our home. We should live for the chance to partake of the feast of happiness, peace, and joy that our loving families grant us for being a grandfather.

Why is it grandfathers sometimes forget they are still dads to their adult children? Daughters still need to feel they are their dad's special princess. Sons still crave the approval from a respected dad. All children have an inner desire to receive praise and acceptance from their father. They want that recognition and nod from a person who is so important in their lives, reaffirming to them they are doing a good job. All of us at any age still have that inner child screaming to our father, like the three-year-old in total excitement trying to get his special attention: "Daddy! Daddy! Daddy! Watch me do this!" And afterward, being so proud of an accomplishment, just radiating with happiness when Dad's attention is captured.

Grandpa G gave me some wise counsel concerning this matter:

> I loved spending time with my grandchildren. I would go grab them and take them different places, the park, the movies, the zoo, the mountains, historical places, the store, for walks, restaurants, swimming, or just to hang out.
>
> I used to often say, "Grandchildren were the reward for being a parent."
>
> After one particularly fun day with the grandchildren, we came back to their home and started to tell their mother, my daughter, about our exciting day. She immediately cut them off in midsentence and walked away. Shocked, we all looked at each other bewildered about her reaction, for it was greatly out-of-character for her. I knew something was wrong, so I followed her. She didn't know I was behind her. As she was walking, I overheard her talking to herself.
>
> She said, "I work hard all day, while they are out playing and having a good time."
>
> Then with a deep sadness in her voice, she exclaimed, "I want to go too—before he was their grandfather, he was my dad. I miss doing things with him."
>
> At that moment, I realized my mistake: there was a certain amount of jealousy, not of her children, but of my time with her. She also wanted to go places with me, to have fun together as daughter and dad. From that time on, we plan time together, just the two of us.
>
> Now one of my favorite sayings is, "My children are my reward for being a parent, and my grandchildren are a plus."

For those fathers who have good healthy relationships with their children, it usually means constant approval and praise from a loving father. Sadly, I talked to several sons and daughters still trying to meet high expectations from a demanding father. To them, the feeling of never being good enough has had a big impact on their lives and personal relationships with spouses and their children. It was very heart-wrenching talking to them as they described the never-ending battle for recognition and acceptance from their fathers.

Do not find fault. Instead, build with uplifting hands, be a friend, a foundation, a helper, a support, not a judge, prosecutor, or an obstacle who adds more burden on already heavy-loaded shoulders. Find ways to lighten the load.

Be a peacemaker. You must share the load duty to the betterment of your children and family, lifting the weights until those who need help gain enough strength to begin again. Be the rock on sound footing, relief from the perils of this world. Your influence can be a counterbalance to the evils of this world. To rebuild structure so they can draw strength and courage from you while developing their own. You must be the life-giving well from which they drink until they can dig their own.

Father and Son Relationships

When you teach your son, you teach your son's son.
—The Talmud

There is no other relationship quite like that which can and should exist between a boy and his dad. It can be one of the most nurturing, joyful relationships in life, one that can have a profound impact on boys who become dads themselves. It will also effect dads who become grandfathers. Now, I understand there are many young men who do not have fathers with whom they could have had the kinds of conversations guiding them through life that are common with fathers and sons. And some men did not have sons or have lost their sons to tragedy or illness. But much of this material will apply to grandfathers and other mentors who sometimes fill the gaps for these significant father-son relationships.

You see, we're all on a journey. Grandfathers are a little farther down the road, but none of us has yet arrived at our final destination. We are all in the process of becoming who we will one day be. Fathers and sons (grandfathers, fathers, and grandsons) can play a critical role in helping each other become the best that they can be.

I know that father-son relationships are never perfect, but if you take some of the suggestions from the chapters of this book, your relationship will become stronger and closer.

Children are a father's pride and joy. In them, grandfathers and fathers see a promising future and their hope for a better version of themselves. Their accomplishments are a joy to grandfathers and fathers. Their worries and problems are grandparents' and parents' worries and problems.

Grandfathers are a primary model of manhood for their sons. You are their most meaningful mentor, and believe it or not, you are their hero in countless ways. Your words and your example are a great influence on both your own sons and grandsons.

As Grandpa G explained to me:

> Each generation learns from the previous generation. Children watch their parents closely, and as they move up in various stages of life, they often pattern after what they saw their own parents do or didn't do.
>
> My father is ninety years old, and I am still learning from him. I am sixty-four. I watched him go through health issues, family concerns, financial ups and downs, and marital problems. Now as I get older, I have had a pioneer of sorts to watch and maybe get some insight into what to expect as I get older.
>
> Seeing his life of pills, naps, forgetfulness, physical limitations, and a healthy attitude for life is teaching me. I am better prepared because of his example and experiences. I still go to him for advice and counsel. Yet

at the same time, I am a grandfather who has children and grandchildren of my own, who are watching me go through those same life experiences, so they in turn will know what are some of the challenges waiting in store for them.

I remember one time talking to my dad when he was in his late fifties, and he was telling me about attending his fortieth-year high school reunion. He said when he got there and started looking around, he was shocked and surprised how everyone seemed so old—a bunch of old men and women! In his mind, the last vision he had of many of them were when they were teenagers.

Thinking about this, that night before he went to bed, he took a hard look for the first time in the mirror and realized he too had aged greatly, becoming an old man.

Now that I am past the age when he had gone to the high school reunion, I too realize I am showing my age, the youthful look is gone. I remembered him saying, "Yet I don't feel as old as I look!" I can relate to his words. Dad told me he had changed so gradually he hadn't even noticed the aging.

Since I first talked to Grandpa G, he had added one more phase about his father after our first interview.

Last week, my dad passed away. The month before his death, we had the chance to spend some time together. As I watched him slowly go through the pain and process of shutting down his life functions, I also saw the peace of moving on to the next phase. Again he was teaching me, not in words, but in example, showing me dignity in such personal final moments without fear or regret.

Father and Daughter Relationships

A son is a son until he takes a wife, but a daughter is a daughter all her life.

—Old Irish Saying

The relationship a daughter has with her father is one that greatly affects her life. This relationship begins in childhood and will continue into adulthood. Regardless if the relationship is healthy or not, it still has some sort of effect on the daughter. Patterns are established as to what a male role is in the mind of a girl, young or old. This pattern will continue throughout the life of a daughter. Countless studies have been performed in regard to daughter-father interactions with all having similar results. Daughters use their fathers as the measuring stick and basis for the values, examples, and standards they'll encounter with all males in their life. Many seek out the same attributes when finding mates. A father's influence continues when the child becomes an adult. The desire for closeness never ends with age between a daughter and her father.

When Gabby Douglas, the Olympics gymnastics gold medalist, was being interviewed by CBS News, one of the questions was about her dad. As the question was asked, you couldn't help but notice a feeling of warmth in her response. Because of her intensive training, which forced her separation from family, and his absence during three tours of duty in the Iraq and Afghanistan wars, she hadn't seen him for some time, but she still felt close to him. She told one reporter, "I just had to pray to God just to keep him safe and tell the angels to keep my dad safe and come home."

During the Olympic trials, her dad made a surprise visit. Gabby told another reporter, "I'm like, 'Who's calling my name?' And then I look up—it was my dad and his friend, and I hadn't seen him in a long time . . . They were holding up the flag. And I almost felt like bawling. I was like, 'Oh my gosh, Dad!'"

A daughter never stops wanting to have her dad be a part of her life. He is . . . her *dad*!

Danielle, a teacher, told me about an experience with one of her coworkers. She had been talking to one of the other teachers at her school, who was expressing an extra amount of joy that day. All of the other coworkers were debating the source of her happiness. Some thought it could have been an award for which she had been nominated. Others thought it might have something to do with her boyfriend and long-term dating partner.

When Danielle was asked about the reason for her elation, she said with a big grin that her dad had called and was coming to visit her. It seems there was a rift in their relationship concerning careers choices, but he had called to try to mend the issue and take her out to dinner.

It dawned on me, by her response, that daughters never stop hungering for their father's attention, love, and approval. Dads can be a huge source of happiness in their daughters' lives. Their dads are their first contact with a male perspective. He is often her hero, protector, and confidant. In a young girl's life, he is either number one or number two of importance. His connection means everything to her.

But sometimes, the father-daughter relationship can be lacking, for many reasons. However, no matter the reason, the question arises, is it too late for fathers who weren't involved in their daughters' lives to make an effort after they have grown up?

Many men operate on that premise—that it might be too late to make a difference. Thinking that the door has been closed because a child has grown must be rethought, because it simply is not true. The door can be reopened. Every daughter has a deep need and hunger for a relationship with a dad. A parent's later involvement in a daughter's world can have a major impact, felt not only by the daughter, but in her children's lives (the grandchildren) as well. The investment will reap tremendous benefits for you and them.

If you find yourself in this situation, here are three suggestions to help with solving the concerns. First, make a list of all the things she has meant to you; be specific and comprehensive. Second, open a line of communication. Be positive, confirming the contributions you have shared together and how she has enriched your life.

Third, take the high road and apologize for any wrongs, no matter who is at fault. Then ask for forgiveness. *Will you forgive me?* and *I am sorry* are powerful words to anyone. Be sincere, and the result can mean a closer, more meaningful relationship with your daughter.

Fourth, ask what you can do to make your relationship better. How can you help her in her life? This will send a message you are willing to submit your time and resources for her betterment.

Remember, the unpleasant occurrences of the past may be erased just like chalk on a chalkboard with real interaction between your children and yourself. Be the one to begin with a new premise and take the first step toward mending the fence between you, no matter how many times you have to take that first step.

For fathers in already healthy relationships: you must continue to participate in activities with your children. Take them out to eat, go to a movie together, watch a sports event, go shopping, or watch a favorite TV show—just you and *one* of your children. Plan a one-on-one adventure you both enjoy. Nourish the association, for the benefit of both of you. And do this with all your grown kids.

Grown Children Revert Back to Being Children

Children become children again when they come home. Remembering their youth, they revert back to it. We all do. In college, I did a paper on behavior patterns of adult children when they returned to their childhood homes to visit parents and siblings. My interviews generated an unexpected result. Childlike symptoms would emerge—playfulness, teasing, and at times, arguments. These adult children would want to be and even encourage being waited on by a mother or father. Age made no difference: eighty-year-olds were serving sixty-year-olds who had grandchildren of their own. Each age group would settle again into the child role while in the home. A pattern was established where each generation would serve their own children, and the children would accept the pampering from their parents.

The project interviews also followed families into their family reunions, concluding with interesting models of behavior. The core family members would congregate to reenact games, activities, and oral stories from when they were young, often leaving spouses to fend for themselves. Each would fall into their familiar role in the family hierarchy, kids in order of birth. Talkers continued to control much of the conversation, while more silent ones remained less talkative. Dominant siblings proceeded to dominate; the rest following their lead. All letting the parents have the final say and input about family matters. The interesting point was the worldly success or failure of the children had no effect on the family's hierarchy or behavior. The less talkative children in the family could have become lawyers or politicians with highly developed verbal skills, yet in their own families, they were still the middle child with less say-so.

One grandpa told about his family reunion with all the children and grandchildren. During one stay at a resort, there was a large swimming pool in which the four *boys* (ages twenty-eight to thirty-six) and dad (in midsixties) started throwing a small, five-inch, football.

Grandpa started to explain.

> Since the boys were little, we would always throw a ball among us, in every possible setting, throughout the home (which Grandma hated)—in the yard, in the park, camping, walking, and in the swimming pool. If there was a ball, we were throwing it. We would make all sorts of games, having different goals or point systems while doing so.
>
> I started throwing a ball to one of my sons in the swimming pool; before long, a second joined in, then a third, and finally the fourth. An old familiar game was initiated, a point system for the most catches. For

the next four hours, the grown boys shoved, pulled, hammered, pushed, and playfully fought for the ball, trying to outdo each other, loving every minute of it. If I could have turned the clock back fifteen years, the smiles, the laugher and camaraderie would have been the same, little boys having fun.

During the game, their wives and children came to interrupt the game—no takers. They were having too much fun doing something long lost in the grownup world. By the time we were through, the evidence of the battle hung heavily on their older bodies. Blistered feet, scratched backs, bruised necks, and battle scars happily earned by their siblings in the name of family competition. The biggest reward for me was seeing them, once again, in full elation of sharing a remembered childhood experience with each other.

Another individual told of the events of another family get-together that took place:

There were three generations in attendance. Lots of food was displayed for all to enjoy, which brought the first level of competition among the sisters of the oldest generation: the judging of the best recipe for the potato salad.

At first it was the pleasant commentaries being exchanged as the judges—husbands, who weren't allowed to rate their own wives' potato salad—began to mark their findings. As each sister's turn came up, a barrage of comments would come out if she scored higher. Finger-pointing started:

"You stole that from Mom."

"You two worked together."

"You had a chef help you."

"You cheated by adding a different ingredient."

All done in a tone of fun and laughter. Before long the sixty- and seventy-year-old grandmas were all at each other, yelling over the competition, just as they did as sisters growing up.

Meanwhile, the sports competition had begun with the brothers again in their sixties and seventies, playing basketball. None of them could run well—just pass, shoot, and harass each other. But they were having fun, like children.

Always remember, your children will forever see you as their dad. They will expect you to be there when they're in trouble and when they have achievements or success, to continue to be a sounding board, and give them the approval that they will constantly crave from you. Deep inside, a part of them will still exist—the feeling of being a child seeking the protected comfort of youth, free of worries.

Chapter 21

These Are Not Your Kids

Your children have to have the chance to make mistakes and grow from them. This includes learning to be a parent. You can't deflect and shield them all the time.

—Grandpa G

A grandfather told me about a lesson he learned when he was new as a grandparent, which set the stage for the rest of his grandparenting future.

As an experienced father, I was used to making decisions, solving problems, and recognizing potentially bad outcomes. This knowledge hadn't come without much trial and error. I had made mistakes as well as successes as a father. But from each, I gained valuable knowledge to make me a better father. If a challenge came up, I could quickly address it, eliminate it, or find a way to deal with it. After raising six children, there wasn't much I couldn't handle.

Being a new grandfather, I thought it would be the same. I would be there to continue to jump in and make decisions, because of my vast knowledge of handling children and family issues.

On this one occasion, my son was disciplining his daughter on some minor infraction of the rules, and upon noticing the hurt look on her face, I was compelled to come to her aid. I jumped in and said something to the effect, "Oh, it wasn't that bad," and "she doesn't need to be punished."

My son immediately stopped, took me by the arm, leading me away out of ear—and eye-range.

He then said, "Dad, I love you, but these are not your children. They are mine. My wife and I will decide how we will raise these children."

It was a sobering message he gave me that day. I realized at that moment, he was right. These were his children, not mine. It was his responsibility to care for, teach, and develop their well-being. I also realized he needed to learn for himself the responsibility of being a father through trial and error, just I had done, as my parents before me. I apologized, and told him he was right. Yet we both knew I would be available for any advice and support he needed, which he took advantage of on many occasions.

But thanks to him, my role as a grandfather has been uplifted. If I see one of my grandchildren do something that creates turmoil within their family, I just smile to myself, mumble "the child is not mine," and watch!

Each gray hair is earned, not given without sacrifice and problems.

Don't misunderstand; offering an opinion only when asked, of course, can be difficult for many grandfathers to accept. But the parent may solicit the grandfather's input in different ways. An adult child might directly ask his father for his opinion concerning a grandchild. Or maybe the grown child will simply open a discussion of the parenting issue involved. In either case, Grandpa, you might feel free to voice an opinion, as long as you use tact.

Here is an example given to me: A teenage grandson has been caught cheating on a test at school. His parents had decided to ground him for a month. Grandpa felt that a month was too long. Maybe the reason for the cheating wasn't addressed correctly in Grandpa's opinion, or maybe he felt the study rules and behavior needed to be further addressed. In this situation, no one knows for certain what was the best solution.

Grandpa's role, when invited, is to open up those areas of his concern for discussion as tactfully as possible. Possibly by *asking questions* about the concerned matters, without making suggestions. The parents will still make the final decision, and he should support that decision, as long as the grandchild is not being abused or mistreated in a way that is clearly harmful to his physical or mental health.

Grandparents have the reputation of being pushovers when it comes to their grandchildren. That desire to be indulgent, however, is tempered by the fact that most grandparents grew up with a different set of expectations than what exists today. All in all, the breadth of our experiences makes us a good source of advice. But advice is hardly ever welcomed, unless it has been asked for, and that's a tough thing for grandparents to remember.

If you want to truly be helpful, Grandpa, keep your mouth shut and your opinions to yourself . . . until they are requested.

One thing Grandpa G did mention passing on to his children for consideration, and I suggest for all grandfathers to propose to their own children for the grandchildren was this: "Bestow big projects, chores, and jobs on children. It will make them better prepared for life, and it will surprise you what they can do. Such as? Organizing the family vacation; handling family finance for three months, paying bills, and ordering food for family and animals; organizing the family schedule or any other major project."

This will help them learn life skill-sets and prepare them for bigger responsibilities, like being a parent as a young adult. If they have been taught how to manage a major chore, then having children might be less challenging.

Just remember, your job is to *support*, not to correct or lecture. The most important question you can ask a parent when in stressful situations is, *"What can I do to help?"* These simple words can be very soothing and lift a weight from burdened shoulders.

One final note: They might not be your children, but your house *is* your home. When children and grandchildren are at your home, make sure you set boundaries for behavior. When boundaries are set, they are usually followed. Where problems arise is often from lack of clarity about what is acceptable and what is not. Establishing boundaries in your home can solve most problems before they occur. This also applies to your children of what they might expect of you and your time. Boundaries can be clarified in a loving and positive manner where all involved can respect them.

Chapter 22

Second Wind

Each new sunrise brings another chance to change your life . . . Gray hairs of experience do not come without a price.

—Grandpa G

The *second wind* is a phenomenon in distance running like marathons or road running whereby an athlete who is too out of breath or too tired to continue suddenly finds the strength to press on at top performance, with less exertion. The feeling may be similar to that of a *runner's high*, the most obvious difference being that the runner's high occurs after the race is over. Being a grandfather in today's world means we have to find that second wind to help us muster the strength to meet the challenges we face every day.

Likewise, we can look at grandfatherhood as a *second chance*. Maybe we weren't able to spend as much time with our own children as we would have liked, or maybe we made some mistakes we now regret. For many, grandchildren represent a fresh start.

In the marathon of life, we have grandfathers who are in family circles outside of the traditional family unit of previous generations. Many grandfathers are single; divorced; in their second, third, or more marriage. A majority of these have step-grandchildren and biological grandchildren from different marriage partners of their own and their children. Some are produced from unmarried partners as well. Our involvement with grandchildren in this environment can range from daily contact to no contact at all. It is important for those of us in these situations to establish the best relationship possible with our grandchildren, not only for ourselves but for the development and well-being of our grandchildren.

Contemporary family configurations can be confusing to our children, our grandchildren, our wives, extended family members, and other siblings. In some households, there might be some jealousy among grandmothers concerning their children versus ours. It is not uncommon to see resentment arise with new wives when it pertains to a grandfathers' time spent with grandchildren.

Unfortunately, there is no easy answer for those in that predicament. Many of the grandfathers I talked to have found, by using some the communication techniques with their wives mentioned here in chapter 14 (*Listen, Listen, Listen*) has helped. But it takes a lot of love, patience, and understanding.

Like starring in a great play, act 1 is done. Think of the changes in your life as the start of act 2. Consider the role as a grandfather as a new beginning, a second chance, to develop better relationships with those you love. This is an opportunity to make life sweeter for you and them. Remember, life never sits still, it is always evolving. There are three things you can always count on—death, taxes, and change.

Grandparenting has evolved into an endeavor with more challenging responsibilities that were not as prevalent in past generations. Nowadays, out of every ten grandparents, one has become the primary caregiver and support of a grandchild at some time in their lives. Nationally, 4.5 million children are living in grandparent-headed households (6.3 percent of all children under age eighteen). This represents a 30 percent increase from 1990 to 2000. Today, the numbers are even higher.[6]

---

6   Pew Research, "Social & Demographics Trends," September 9, 2010.

Kinship caregivers, particularly grandparents, face a variety of emotional, legal, and daily-living challenges as they unexpectedly find themselves in the position of raising a second family. Many factors contribute to the dramatic increase in the number of kinship-care families, including:

divorce	debilitating disease
death	incarceration
teenage pregnancy	drug and alcohol abuse

Becoming a caregiver can happen suddenly, and it is often very difficult to adjust to the changes that occur. The extra time that is needed often means spending less time and attention with other people in your life. It is common for caregivers and their friends to feel they no longer share common interests with each other. Priorities change; instead of being able to schedule time on the golf course or have lunch with a friend, children take precedent. Being responsible for young children will transform the decision making of how a person will spend time. Grandparents and friends may feel some discomfort having children with them in certain social situations. In spite of these changes, there are ways to maintain healthy relationships.

Strong relationships take a lot of work. Taking on the responsibility of a child should be planned together with each member of the family. Having additional children in your life can create a tremendous strain on your relationship with your spouse . . . on so many levels. It affects your lifestyle, emotional solidity, finances, and sexual relationship. Marriage has enough challenges without accepting more responsibility by having grandchildren move in with you.

When a grandparent suddenly must become the parent, there are often profound feelings of disappointment and even anger toward the irresponsible behavior of the grandchild's parent. Such feelings can often lead to a strained relationship between the caregiver and the grown child. Understandably, this is typically not in the best interests of the grandchild, particularly if there is going to be an ongoing relationship with the child's parent or parents.

The hardest part is establishing a structured home in which children can feel safe, receive love, have stability, and be assured in their lives. Children need routines, patterns, goals, and discipline to feel good about themselves. They want to be part of a family unit. If it isn't available with their own parents then it falls upon the shoulders of the grandparents. This reassures them and provides peace of mind to their young minds and spirits.

It isn't an easy role to fulfill. It is normal for children to miss their parents and want to be taken care of by them. The feeling of abandonment or loss can weigh heavy on their hearts. They might question themselves, "What if I had done or said something different; would there have been a different outcome?" Find ways for them to constructively express their feelings of anger or hurt.

Your relationship is primary in creating the foundation for you, your spouse, and the grandchildren. Remember the little things that show you care, such as hugs and kisses; a thank-you both to grandchildren and your spouse goes a long way during stressful times. Small things mean a lot. Show kindness, patience, love, and forgiveness.

The other family members, such as your other children and grandchildren, may feel jealous of the time and attention given to the children in your care. Some of your own children may feel it is unfair to spend more of your resources of time and money on the other siblings and their children. It may also apply to relationships you have with friends outside of the family who feel you have abandoned the relationship for lack of time and resources. If those feelings exist with others (family or friends), they may never express them directly to you, creating even more stress. The best solution is constant communication with those you care about. Ask for their advice. Bring them into your circle. There is no easy answer.

Friends, family, neighbors, church members, and so on can be powerful sources of support. If they are not able to help, they might know someone who can. Make contact with others via support groups. Support groups are created to help their participants better cope with issues caused by the situation.

Try to keep humor in your life. Humor is always appreciated and even welcomed to lighten situations and relieve stress. It is like finding the coveted prize in your bowl of cereal. It changes your day.

A grandfather gave me this story about a wife who was raising grandchildren in her home:

> The grandmother was getting dinner, when the phone rang. The school nurse was calling to tell her that her grandson had come down with a high fever and she needed to come get him to bring him home.
>
> After figuring the time it would take to drive to school and back, and how long the dinner would take if she put it in the oven, she concluded there was enough time. She then left for school. When she arrived, her grandson's fever was worse, and it was obvious she would have to take him directly to the urgent care.
>
> During his examination the doctor told her she needed to get some medicine as quickly as possible and she should get him into bed right away. Feeling some panic, she rushed home and put him in bed, then ran back out to go get his medicine. Feeling more pressure, she had totally forgotten about the dinner. At the drug store, she got the prescription filled and rushed back to the car to find it was locked.
>
> Sure enough, the keys were inside the car. Using her phone, she tried to call her husband, but he was in a meeting and unavailable. Next, she called her grandson at home, just in case her husband would call. Being more frustrated, she exclaimed she had locked the keys in the car. Not feeling well, her grandson, whispered, "Grandma, get a wire coat hanger to get into the car." Then he hung up.
>
> So back to the drug store she went to find a wire hanger. No luck; there were only wood and plastic hangers. The same was true in the other stores in the

strip mall, no wire hangers to be found. Finally, in a discount used-items store, she found a wire coat hanger.

Thinking to herself, she thought, What am I going to do with this hanger?

Panicking, she tried to call her grandson, but her cell phone battery had died. Overcome with failure, she dropped to her knees and began crying.

Then she prayed, "Dear Lord, my grandson is sick, and he needs this medicine, and I need to finish the dinner; plus, the keys are locked in the car and, Lord, I don't know what to do with this coat hanger. Dear Lord, send somebody who does know what do with it, and I really need that person *now*, Lord. Amen."

At that moment, she looked up and saw a young man walking toward her, who was dressed in faded jeans and a worn-out shirt, with tattooed arms, a beard and unruly hair. Jumping in front of him, showing him the wire hanger, she asked, "Could you open my locked car with this?"

Surprised at first, he then said, "No problem, where is the car?"

At the car, he used the hanger to maneuver around the window and, with a quick flick of the hanger, the car door popped right open. In less than thirty seconds, he accomplished the task.

With the car door open, she couldn't contain herself and threw her arms around him and said, "You must be a good and Godly man, for the Lord must have sent you."

Jumping back, he said, "No ma'am, I'm neither Godly nor a good man. I just got out of prison yesterday."

Hugging him again, she exclaimed, "Bless the Lord! He sent me a professional!"

Remember you are not alone. Use all your resources; help will be there.

Chapter 23

Memorable Moments That Last Forever

There is a story given to me from a grandfather of a young boy anxiously waiting for his granddad to get home from work.

"Grandpa, how much do you earn in an hour?" the little grandson asked.

Surprised by the question, the grandpa responded, "I don't know exactly. I will have to figure it out."

"Grandpa, please tell me! How much do you make an hour?" the little boy insisted.

After thinking about it for a moment, Grandpa said, "Around twenty dollars an hour."

"Great, Grandpa. Could you loan me ten dollars?" the boy asked.

A little bewildered, Grandpa asked, "Is this the reason you asked me how much I make, so you can ask for money? Maybe you should go to bed, and we can talk about it in the morning."

Later, after he was settled in, Grandpa started reflecting on the earlier conversation and began to feel somewhat guilty. Maybe he should have found more about what the boy wanted to buy. Finally, to ease his mind, Grandpa decided to go to his grandson's room.

Grandpa asked, "Are you asleep, son?"

"No, Grandpa. Why?" replied the boy, half asleep.

"I have brought you the money you asked for earlier," Grandpa said.

"Thank you, Grandpa! I now have enough money, twenty dollars!" The little child said to his Grandpa as he put it under his pillow.

Looking at his grandson, feeling a little confused, he questioned, "Enough for what?"

Staring into his grandfather's eyes, the little boy responded, "Grandpa, can you sell me one hour of your time?"

This example amplifies the desire of our grandchildren wanting us to share time with them. Each child has a need to be special. Sharing activities, including a variety of functions or events directed at their level of acceptance, makes them feel important. A common theme in all the surveys from both children and grandfathers was directly related to the amount of time expended with each other. For grandfathers, it was regret for not spending enough time, and for children, it was being thankful for the chance to receive the time they did have together.

Another grandfather told me about this experience with his five-year-old granddaughter.

> I had just had some cancer surgery and was staying at my son's home during the recovery. It took a long year before I could move out on my own. During that time I had time to interact with my grandchildren on a daily basis. It was wonderful to be part of the family. I had grown extremely close to my little granddaughter, who had just turned five. One day, I returned to visit and was met with the biggest hugs and outpouring of love—even the dog was all over me.
>
> At the end of the visit, as I was saying my good-byes, my little five-year-old came up and put her little arms around me and asked, "Grandpa are you going to move back in with us? I missed you so much!" she said.
>
> "No, dear, I have my own place now, but I will come to visit you often," he responded.

> Dropping her head and then looking up with a pouty face and the saddest eyes that only a small child can convey, she said, "Grandpa, I know you will visit, but it isn't the same as having you here all the time. I love and miss you so much."

Creating memorable moments for a grandchild only happens by spending time with them. You will never know what will be remembered as a cherished memory and what will be discarded, never to be remembered. You will never know when or what will be a memorable moment. If you try to plan for the perfect teaching opportunity, it will never work out. Children have their own ways of remembering what is important to them. The common denominators are always shared time and making the child feel special.

How a Child Spells Love: T-I-M-E

The following were some of the treasured occasions passed on to me by grandchildren in the surveys. I was surprised at what they remembered. But what they did remember will be with them forever, often told and retold to their children.

The following stories were stimulated by responses from two questions in the survey:

"What do you remember about your grandfather?"

"What was the best time you had with him?"

Each story is self-explanatory.

Talking While Hammering Nails

The best time I remember about Grandpa was when we were hammering nails into a stump when I was little. If you were to ask me why, it was because we just talked as he showed me how to use a hammer, pounding them in and pulling nails out of the stump. I know it probably didn't mean as much to him, but to me, using that big hammer, beating on those nails, and us talking about all sorts of things made me feel special. I will never forget that day, even though I was very young.

Such a simple thing, yet it made a big impact. Many of the stories all come back to a memorable time when the child got special attention and was made to feel important.

Grandfather's House for Thanksgiving

Every year, our family would go Grandpa's and Grandma's house for Thanksgiving. It was fun seeing all the cousins, aunts, and uncles. The big highlight was when Grandpa would hitch up the large wagon to the tractor and load all of the grandchildren in and take us to the small river down below his farm. We would play in the water and find all sorts of things to entertain ourselves while Grandpa would talk to us. But the thing I liked the most was coming back, because Grandpa would let me ride on the tractor with him while all the rest rode in the wagon. Girls never got to ride on the tractor, only the boys. So to be selected the granddaughter to ride with him was a big deal to me. Grandpa didn't say much, but I felt good, because I got to always go with him on the tractor. He died before I was a teenager.

Flying with Grandpa

Grandpa was a pilot. He had his own plane and would fly it whenever he could get out of the house. Grandma would tell us to be sure to keep the door shut, or Grandpa would escape to go flying.

One of his favorite items to fly was a glider. The only problem was, when he was going to fly the glider, he had to have a second person in the glider with him to help with the system. From when I was an early age, he started asking me to go with him. Grandma had gotten tired of going, and my parents were all too busy. Thus, we became flying buddies. It was fantastic. Whenever he was going flying he would call to see if I could go.

For years, we flew all over Rockies, discovering all sorts of hidden places in the mountains. We flew for hours, looking down below. The best part of our adventures was we had time to talk. Our discussions were endless, and to a preteen, then later a teenage girl, it was heaven. He always listened and helped me to understand things my parents didn't have time to talk about. He showed me how to fly and to see things from a different point of view. Grandpa and I had an exclusive connection, which I will hold dear to my heart forever.

Talking Over a Shovel

As a teenager, my parents used to send me every summer to work on the farm with Grandpa. He was starting to get up there in years, and they would send me to help him. For me, being from the city, it was without a doubt, a different experience. I had no idea how hard it was to work on a farm. The early morning wakeup calls, breakfast before the sun was up, long hours with all sorts of chores was a rude awakening to me. At first, I hated the concept when my dad proposed it to me. I was looking forward to spending time with my friends and hanging out with them during the summer. But I knew my grandfather needed help, so I agreed.

It turned out to be the best decision of my life. Working with my grandfather allowed me to learn so much about him and our family. We traveled around in his 1960 pickup, bouncing on those dusty dirt roads. He would point out places where historical events had happened near the farm.

I learned how to work hard, especially lifting and stacking those 110-pound bales of hay. However, the time I grew closest with him was during irrigation duties. Each summer, we would have to build and clean out irrigation ditches to water the crops. After finishing the digging, we would stand over our shovels monitoring the flow of water and just talk. Maybe it was because we were so tired and didn't want to move, with sweat coming down our faces, covered in dust, but those were special moments for me. We discussed everything from politics to world events, morals, religion, family, and desirable standards. He valued my opinions, thoughts, and always was encouraging me, yet never judging. He treated me as an equal, not just a grandson. I loved those summers on the farm with Grandpa.

The Orange Bronco Chair

We visited Grandpa and Grandma one year during the football season. Grandpa was an avid Denver Broncos fan. He loved his Broncos. While we were there, his favorite reclining chair was broken by us children during a particular rowdy game of wrestling. Because there were several of us visiting and staying at the home, another chair was needed in the family room. So Grandpa decided to go look for a chair. He asked me to go with him. We visited several discount stores, Goodwill and others. Finally when we were about to give up, Grandpa said, "Let's try one more store."

Like most used or second-hand stores, there wasn't much to choose from. As we were about leave, I saw a reclining chair in the book section, put there to allow readers a place to sit down. I told Grandpa about it.

Now I wasn't very old, maybe nine or ten, so I didn't know anything about colors, matching furniture, or different furniture styles, I just saw a chair I liked. We walked over to inspect it. It was in pretty good shape, and the price tag was only forty dollars. There was only one problem: it was . . . bright orange. It was so orange you had to cover your eyes so as not to get hurt looking at it! Grandpa, who sensed my enthusiasm and pride in finding the chair, sat in it to try it out. I think more to please me than entertaining the idea of really buying it.

However, once he sat down . . . he said, "Wow, this is a very comfortable chair."

He decided if he could talk them down some on the price, he would buy it. Grandpa told me if he could get it for twenty bucks, it would be worth it to use the chair for the holidays while everyone was there in the home. After the holidays, he would probably throw it away.

I enjoyed watching Grandpa haggle with the clerk, hoping he could get the price down. I thought Grandpa was the best haggler ever. Finally the clerk agreed: he would sell it for the price of twenty dollars. (As I have gotten older, I think the clerk was happy to get rid of that old orange chair.)

When we got home, I was so proud of making the "find of the century" with Grandpa. We took it into the house, beaming about our purchase for only twenty dollars, but when Grandma saw it, all hell broke loose.

"You are not bringing that ugly chair in my house. What were you thinking?" she yelled.

Now, Grandma is a very formidable woman who was used to getting her way, especially concerning anything pertaining to the house.

After looking at me, I then noticed a determined, hard look come over Grandpa's face.

He said, "Woman, your grandson picked this chair out. It stays!"

"We will see," she muttered, walking away.

I couldn't believe it—Grandpa stood up for me in front of Grandma. That was major to a young boy, me. Grandpa had just become my hero.

Turning to me, he said, "I think we will name it the Bronco Chair, because it matches one of the colors on the Denver Broncos uniform—orange."

Grandpa kept that recliner for many years, right in the middle of the family room. It never matched anything. Grandma hated it. Whenever somebody would ask about it, Grandpa would relate the story how we found the Bronco Chair. On all our visits, I got to sit in the Bronco Chair.

Finally Grandma convinced Grandpa to replace it. Much later, the Bronco Chair was moved to my uncle's room and used for a long time by him watching the games. When he got older, and moved out of their house, I took it.

The wood handle was broken, so I used a wrench instead. The fabric had many frayed edges, but no tears. There were several stains from spilled pop, chips, and various food items, yet it still maintained its comfort. Most of all, it reminded me of Grandpa, particularly the day he stood up to Grandma for me.

Birthday Shopping at Walmart

Since Grandpa got divorced, he wasn't very good at remembering birthdays. Sometimes he would call, send a card or give a present; other times, he just forgot. Then one year, he came up with a plan for me and my three siblings. Each year during one of his visits, he would take us to Walmart and let us pick out anything we wanted under twenty-five dollars. And this would be our birthday present for the year.

"Does this mean one item or as many items as we can buy up to twenty-five dollars?" I asked him.

"Whatever you want—you are free to buy anything, but you must spend twenty-five dollars," Grandpa said.

It was so much fun, as each of us was trying to figure out the seemingly endless combinations of toys, candy, and books. Each year, we would go from aisle to aisle searching, pricing, and trying to discover the perfect items. We would share our baskets of treasures with each other, asking for advice and suggestions before the final checkout. Oh, the excitement it was for us! Just think, whatever we wanted, without our parents saying yes or no. It was heavenly.

Even today, I sometimes wish I could go through the aisles and pick out anything I wanted, without feeling guilty or saying to myself "you don't need that, put it back." Shopping at Walmart with Grandpa was pure joy.

Camping in the Rocky Mountains

When I was eleven Grandpa came to visit us. During the visit, he mentioned to my mom and dad about going fishing at his favorite spot high in the mountains near the town Leadville, Colorado. Grandpa asked if my dad wanted to go. Grandpa had taken my mom several times when she was young, but my dad had never been to the isolated lake. Unfortunately, dad said he couldn't get away due to work obligations, but dad turned, pointed at me, and asked Grandpa if he wanted to take me instead. At that point, Mom interrupted to say that she wasn't comfortable about taking me up to the secluded lake. She continued with her concerns: the two-and-a-half-mile backpacking route, with the last quarter mile virtually straight up; it was the first of October, when the snows could come at any day on the high mountain tops, sealing in the trails for winter.

Both Dad and Grandpa pleaded with my mom, saying how this would be a great opportunity for me that may not come again and that I was big for my age, which would allow me to meet the physical demands of the trip. Reluctantly, Mom agreed to let me go, with the condition that at the first sign of snow we would pack up and leave.

I was so excited, for I had heard many stories about this lake from Grandpa. The fish were plentiful. It was full of native trout: brownies, brook, and rainbow. He would say that his arms would get tired from reeling them in to shore. My favorite story was about the time he caught four fish with one cast. After casting the line out into the water with his fly for bait, a small fish immediate took the fly. While reeling it in, another bigger fish swallow the first fish as he got it near the shore. When he put the net under the two fish, the bigger fish let go of the first small fish and fell into the net. Just then another large fish tried to swallow the now freed smaller first fish. The strain of the two fish tugging on the line caused the fly to dislodge from the small fish's mouth, leaving both fish to fall into the net. Now there were three fish in the net. When the fly flipped out of the small fish's mouth, it dropped on top of the water, attracting another fish that took the fly, thus having four fish on one cast. When Grandpa told the story, it was so funny and entertaining.

Grandpa had an older Jeep he would take whenever he went into the mountains. He said we would take it up to the base of the trail instead of his pickup truck. The Jeep still had the summer bikini top on it, which only covered the top part, leaving the back and sides open, without doors. Mom asked Grandpa if we shouldn't change to the heavier top since it was October in the mountains, when weather can change at anytime. Grandpa told Mom that the weather was still warm—in the 70s—and we wouldn't need to put on the full, enclosed top. Big mistake! How do moms always know? The next day, with our backpacks and gear, we headed out in Grandpa's Jeep. The trip through the mountains was about three hours from our home.

Because of a delayed start, we arrived late in the afternoon at the spot where we would leave the Jeep parked at the base of the mountain trail. Grandpa decided that we would stay the night so we could get an early start on the two-and-a-half-mile trail up to the lake. The place where we chose to camp that night was near a beaver dam on a small stream. After setting up camp, including tents, sleeping bags, cooking gear, and lanterns, we decided to go visit the beaver dam. The dam was amazing and beautiful. The way the beavers had interweaved the branches and logs to form a dam yet still allowing water to flow beyond the dam was quite an engineering feat. Grandpa pointed out all the workings of the dam, where beavers worked and the location of their home. The beavers apparently did not like us there, because they would slap their tails at us, making a big racket that echoed through the canyon. Grandpa explained how the water behind the dam was deeper than one expects; in this small stream, it was over ten feet deep. I told Grandpa it was one of the most beautiful places I had ever seen. Then Grandpa said this place was nothing compared to the hidden lake up the canyon. I could hardly wait to see the lake.

For dinner, Grandpa had brought some steaks and had decided to cook them over the campfire. I thought it was so cool, just like mountain men high in the Rockies. I don't think any steak ever tasted as good.

After dinner we sat around the campfire dodging the smoke as the wind changed directions. Our clothes soon began to smell of smoke and bug spray, as we had a few mosquitoes buzzing around us looking for an open spot to attack. During this time, Grandpa and I just sat and talked. He told stories of his youth and our family. We discussed what was happening in my life, its challenges and successes. It was wonderful to talk one on one alone with Grandpa in the wilderness, without the distractions that are constantly fighting for our time and attention. We had a chance to really connect.

As the hours passed and we noticed it was getting colder, Grandpa told me to bundle up when I went to bed because it felt like we might be facing lower temperatures during the night. It turned out that Grandpa was right; the temperature did drop, and I had sunk deep into my sleeping bag in a tight little ball to stay warm.

When I woke up in the morning, all was quiet and still. The sides of my tent were pushed in about five inches. I then heard Grandpa coming out of his tent to say we had gotten some snow. I quickly dressed, and then unzipped my tent and saw it was snowing with four to five inches of fresh snow on the ground. This changed everything Grandpa had said. The trail up on top would have at least a foot or more of snow. The trail would be closed for the winter. Seeing my disappointment, Grandpa mentioned that maybe we could go for a short hike after breakfast. Once we finished a breakfast of hot cocoa and hot cereal, we broke down camp and loaded everything into the Jeep, which was covered with snow inside and out.

The snow was continuing to fall, and the temperature was dropping. But since Grandpa had promised to take me for a short hike, we started out. Walking in the mountains with valleys and thick forest can be disorienting and even more so when snow covers potential landmarks used as references. We hadn't gone more than a quarter mile when we realized we weren't sure where the Jeep was located. Now Grandpa said we weren't lost but just confused as to the right direction that would get us back to the Jeep the fastest.

By this time I was getting scared, but Grandpa said to not to worry about it, for we could always follow our footprints in the snow back to the Jeep. Looking down at our tracks as the snow was coming down in bigger flakes and quickly covering our footprints, I knew we would be in big trouble if we didn't move fast. Grandpa realized it too. So we started running following our old tracks. Now the tracks were being covered and the visibility was down to 20 feet. It had become a blizzard situation. We ran faster, finally the tracks were gone. Not sure where to go we just stood there, trying to get our wits about us. At that moment grandpa thought he saw a little red spot through the trees. Moving closer we realized with great relief we had found the Jeep. Snow had gotten so heavy on the Jeep's back reflector that it had just fallen off exposing a reflector at the moment when grandpa was looking in that direction. It was miracle, because the rest of the Jeep was completely covered in snow. I don't know if we would have found it otherwise.

We weren't out of trouble yet, after getting the snow out of the Jeep so we could sit down we headed out on a road which by that time had 12 plus inches of snow on it. The dirt road was very hard to distinguish hidden under the snow. Meanwhile the temperature was still dropping to near freezing. Finally, after very agonizing moments we managed to get to a hard surfaced or paved road. However, with the open Jeep we couldn't go very fast because it was too cold. I have never been that cold, ever. The freezing wet wind blowing in on us chilled us to the bone. The heater wasn't affective because there was no doors, sides or back on the Jeep. We couldn't talk because our teeth were involuntarily chattering, it seemed our whole bodies were shaking while fighting snow and cold. Our hair had icicles on it, much like you see on the beards of the adventures who go to the north or south poles. It took us nearly 2 hours to get to a low enough elevation before we could breathe without hurting our lungs. We were a mess when we pulled in our driveway. The Jeep was still full of snow our clothes and grear were all frozen. Mom who was extremely worried saw us pull into the driveway came running up to us to see if we were alright. Upon verifying I was ok she gave grandpa the look only a woman can do of disapproval almost stating, what the heck grandpa.

Grandpa just looked at her and said this was a great adventure for your son. It is a story we will always remember and tell. For it is the hard times people go through which are treasured memories and not forgotten while easy times soon disappear unremembered and lost. Then grandpa just smiled at her and so did I.

Golfing with Grandpa

Going golfing with Grandpa was so much fun. The first time I went with Grandpa, I was about seven or eight years old. He let me ride with him on the golf cart. It was so much fun riding with him. He made sure I had a good time. I know he wasn't supposed to, but he would chase birds, rabbits, and my uncles. Nothing was safe on the course. He would even let me drive sometimes, and for an eight-year-old nothing was greater.

One time, Grandpa picked up my dad on the front of the golf cart and told him he would take him over to his ball. My dad's golf cart was being used across the course with my uncle Mike who had hit a ball wide, off the fairway. While my dad was hanging on the cart for dear life, Grandpa really pushed the pedal down, Grandpa looked at me, smiling, and said, "Watch this."

This was one of his favorite sayings, and it quickly became one of mine, because I knew something exciting was about to happen whenever he said "watch this."

Once dad was on the cart, Grandpa headed straight for the sprinklers—my poor dad didn't have a chance. Grandpa drove the golf cart right into the middle of the sprinklers, soaking my dad from head to toe. I never laughed so much in my entire life. Even now, when I think of it, I still have to smile, remembering my dad yelling, trying to hold on, and Grandpa practically falling over, laughing so hard.

The account I loved the most while golfing with Grandpa happened later, when I was about fourteen. We were at a golf course where the first starting tee was positioned in front of the restaurant, which had big glass windows. Golfers sitting in the restaurant would watch other golfers as they hit the ball from the tee to begin their play. It was early afternoon, so the restaurant was full from the morning golfers who had finished their rounds.

We had a little delay before it was our turn to start. Grandpa was taking a few practice swings with his driver; then all a sudden, he got this big grin on his face. He looked at me and said, "Watch this."

He grabs something out of his bag and walks over in front of the restaurant, facing the restaurant, and puts a golf ball on a tee. Grandpa then proceeds to take a couple of big practice swings, aiming directly at the restaurant. Now, I am wondering what he is doing. I noticed I wasn't alone with this thought. The folks in the restaurant were all watching also. Everyone had quit eating anxiously watching Grandpa. I could see the puzzlement and some fear on their faces. As if they were thinking, "What is this idiot getting ready to do?"

Then Grandpa extended his arm with the golf club pointing it toward the restaurant, basically telling them "look out; it is coming your way." It reminded me of a baseball player pointing to centerfield as if to promise a homerun

Now, I saw real panic among the diners within the room. Grandpa took his time, approached the ball, lined it up, looked at the restaurant window, glanced back at the ball, smiled, then took a big backswing and swung forward with all his might. The golf ball took off like a rocket hurdling toward the glass window.

Inside the restaurant became a place of pandemonium. Golfers were dodging for cover, chairs overturned, and small screams of terror uttered. I was in shock, thinking what have you done, images racing through my head of police and unpleasant problems. Then while in this state of uncertainty, I happened to notice the golf ball Grandpa hit. It was a whiffle ball—the plastic kind that has holes throughout! The ball flew fast and furious for several feet before dropping harmlessly to the ground, about halfway between Grandpa and the restaurant. Grinning, Grandpa sauntered over to pick up his ball.

Then he begins to laugh, and so did I. Looking inside, there was a bunch of angry looks, but I believe I even saw a few smiles on the faces of the golfers in the restaurant. Yep, it was fun going golfing with Grandpa. We had some delightful times and conversations on the golf course.

Grandpa's Schooling

I once asked Grandpa how much formal schooling he had attended. He said he had graduated from the fourth grade but got his diploma from the school of hard knocks. Continuing, "And I have earned several degrees from the school." He then pointed to a small two-inch scar on his cheek, then said, "This one came from wire-breaking and flipping, causing a deep gash in my face when I was stringing fence wire while in a hurry to be somewhere else—not taking the proper time to be careful." Pointing to his crooked wrists, he said, "These came from reins I was holding while sleeping in the carriage—when the horses were spooked, snapping my wrist—instead of paying attention."

Showing me a set of scars on his side, all lined up in a row, "This degree was earned as my brother and I were wrestling in the barn instead of pitching hay to the hungry animals. I tripped and fell on the pitch fork." Then smiling, he pointed to the middle of his chest and said, "This was earned when Sally Hutchinson moved away, breaking my heart."

Grandpa saw everything in black and white. He lived by simple rules and stuck to them. He had a handmade sign in his home, which I believed that he'd patterned his life upon. He once told me if you do these things you will be happy and successful.

The sign read, "If it is right, do it. If it is wrong, don't do it. If you're not sure, don't do it. Don't lie. Don't cheat. Show respect, love, and be faithful to your spouse. Help others when they need it. Go to church. Pray to your maker morning and evening. Teach your children through patience, love, and discipline. Show respect to all men."

Grandpa and His Chevy Truck

Grandpa had an old Chevy truck built in the forties or fifties. He loved the truck. He knew every part of the truck. He was always fixing and tuning it. He used to tell me, "On the farm, you don't have the luxury of going into town to have things repaired; you had to learn to do everything yourself." I believed Grandpa could fix anything. It seemed like he was constantly working on something. His wardrobe consisted of two sets of overalls—one for cold days and one for warmer days.

Grandpa was always in his truck with a full assortment of tools, wire, duct tape, rags, oils, a shovel, guns, and parts. I don't know how many miles were on the truck, but he had it for well over forty years. Rust had taken its bite out the sides and floorboard. On the driver's side, Grandpa had put a heavy-duty floor mat to cover a huge hole. It was so big, I could climb through it to get out of the truck. Grandpa used to always say he had three brakes in his truck: "the pedal brake, the hand brake, and the manual foot brake," which implied he could remove the mat and use his feet to stop the truck. Every time I see a Flintstone cartoon, I think of Grandpa using his feet to start and stop his truck.

Raccoon Hunting with Grandpa

When I was about twelve, Dad and Mom decided to visit Grandpa in his home in Missouri. He had a small farm, where he raised turkeys. His farm was surrounded by heavy brush and "woods," as my mom used to call them. Since we were from eastern California, with wide-open spaces and sparse, desert landscape, I didn't know much about thick groups of trees or dense woods. On his farm, Grandpa had several dogs. I guess everyone had dogs on their farms back there. One day, he was telling my dad how he had been training his dogs to raccoon hunt, or as Grandpa would simply say "go coon hunting."

Realizing that my dad hadn't ever been raccoon hunting with dogs before, Grandpa suggested that maybe Dad might want to go on a hunting outing. Then pointing at me, Grandpa said, "We can bring the boy, even though he might be a little young since usually you need to be a little older to go."

Dad responded, "He is a bit young, but big for his age . . . we had better ask his mom, since she knows what is involved during the hunt." My heart was racing, wanting to go so badly.

When we went inside the house to ask Mom if I could go, she looked at them, "Are you kidding me? He is too young. No!" she said.

I was dejected.

Seeing my disappointment, Grandpa said to Mom, "Come on, Maudie, he will be fine; let him come. I will take good care of him."

"Like you did with my brother Bill, who came home from raccoon hunting with a broken arm due to falling out of the tree?" she stated.

Ignoring her statement, "This may be the only chance he will get to go," he pleaded.

For several minutes, Grandpa kept pestering Mom about me going with him. He wasn't going to stop. To avoid the barrage of constant verbal attack, Mom finally gave me permission to go.

I could hardly contain my excitement, I was so happy! This would be my first hunting trip. Yet I had no idea what to expect.

We loaded the dogs and a cage into the truck and headed out into some remote area of the woods. Grandpa prepared the dogs and suggested Dad build a fire.

A fire, why did we need a fire? I wondered. Aren't we going to run after the dogs? I had seen fox-hunting on a TV program where they chased behind as the hounds ran through the landscape in hot pursuit of the fox. I had imagined it would be something along the same procedure. A fire . . . I was confused.

A few minutes later, Grandpa released the dogs. They took off running in two directions, barking like crazy. Then Grandpa brought out some fold-up chairs, food, drinks, and we began to sit around the fire.

What?

I couldn't control my enthusiasm any longer, "Grandpa aren't we going to chase after the dogs?" I asked him.

"Well . . . we will . . . all in good time, son, but for now, we will rest and let the dogs do their work," he replied.

We sat there for some time while Grandpa told us what was going on with the dogs. He knew each bark and what they meant. "Ole Roger has got the trail, and now Sammy is joining him in the chase . . . uh oh, young Blueboy just found a skunk . . ." For almost an hour, we listened to the sounds of the barking dogs running through the woods hot on the trail of a raccoon.

The dogs were in unison now, chasing the raccoon, Grandpa told us. "It won't be long now." A short time later, the barking sounds changed; there was a new bark heard coming from the dogs while gathered at the same spot. Grandpa got up and announced, "We had better get going. Those dogs have treed the raccoon."

Off we went through the brush toward the dogs. We must have walked half a mile to get to the place where the dogs were located. Once there, Grandpa pointed to the raccoon up in the tree. "Yeah, there he is, out on that branch."

Dad asked Grandpa, "How do we get him down?"

"We shoot him, right?" I suggested.

"No, we need to trap him. So someone needs to go up there and get him out of the tree. I am too old, and he is too heavy," Grandpa said, pointing at my dad while smiling knowingly at me.

I knew where this was going. I thought, I am not going up that tree. Sure enough, a few minutes later, I am climbing the tree, heading toward the raccoon.

As I started to move toward the raccoon, now on the same branch, it dawned on me I had no idea what was I going to do when I got near him. Just then, the raccoon started snarling and baring his teeth at me; it was the biggest raccoon I had ever seen.

Oh crap. I thought I was dead, hanging on to that small branch twenty feet in the air. I am going to fall and break something just like my uncle Bill did. Nevertheless, I continued inching my way toward the cornered animal while trying to control my fear. I knew I had to face it, because my dad and

Grandpa were watching me, so I felt I couldn't disappoint them. Then, the raccoon started coming toward me fast, with its teeth showing. With nowhere to go, I rolled over, frantically hanging on the underside of the branch, almost losing my grip, but somehow the raccoon shot right pass me, leaving me unscathed. The raccoon came down the tree, and the dogs cornered him, allowing Grandpa to capture him and put him in the cage.

Grandpa told me how proud he was of me, and he knew it took a lot of courage to go out on that limb with the wild animal. Most boys my age would have been too afraid to do it.

It was a night I will never forget. I am so thankful Grandpa talked Mom into letting me go.

Through the years, as I have faced many situations where I had to face difficult challenges, I will draw from that experience of being on that limb that night, receiving encouragement from Grandpa, and I will find the courage to meet each of my wild animals with confidence.

Sour Oranges from Grandpa G

Grandpa G would come to visit us each winter, bringing gifts from his citrus tree, including grapefruit, lemons, tangerines, and oranges. Among the oranges would be his special variety, sour oranges. He explained to us that all of the citrus trees in Arizona come from the same trunk base. The trees are all sour orange trees. Normal citrus trees can't grow in the hot desert environment. So all young citrus trees are grafted with limbs from other types of fruit, causing their fruit to change from the natural or original sour orange tree into a sweeter fruit. It is even possible to graft into the main trunk more than one fruit, such as tangerines and oranges, creating a tree with both fruit types on the same tree. If the tree freezes back to its original state or is not grafted with a different fruit, it will produce a sour, bitter-orange fruit.

Many homeowners have sour orange trees for aesthetics, while enjoying the sweet smell when the orange blossoms are in bloom. The sour oranges, when cut up into slices, look just as juicy and delicious as a normal orange.

Grandpa G would have us invite friends over for some fresh oranges. Of course, we loved to see our friends bite into the sour oranges, expecting the sweet taste of orange, instead having their taste buds and palate hit with a bolt of sourness. Their mouths would pucker, eyes squint, face contorting, and then look at us in bewilderment. It was funny. Grandpa G loved doing that every year.

River-Rafting on the Arkansas River—Grandpa Said, "It Will Be the Experience of a Lifetime"

One year, Grandpa came up with the idea to take me rafting on the Arkansas River in Colorado. I was twelve years old and full of energy. The opportunity to go river-rafting filled my mind with a high-adventure prospect, riding in the raft, navigating through treacherous rapids, having water spraying in my face, bobbing up and down as we paddled our way down the river. I envisioned following the footsteps of the great explorers, as they had done in years past. At twelve, I could have the chance to conquer the river.

My mother didn't see the same vision I had.

She saw a boy being knocked out of the raft, smashing into rocks, swimming for his life as he was dragged down the river by the swift current, out of control. Her answer was simply, NO. She said I was too young to go in that section of the river. She said there were too many dangerous class 3 and class 4 rapids there.

I was devastated. My dream was gone.

She suggested, "Why don't you take a canoe trip on a calmer river like the Platte or Green River, or take the canoe to the Chatfield Lake?"

Grandpa countered, "Because it isn't as much fun. The boy needs some excitement and challenges in his life. This would give him the opportunity to see and do things he normally wouldn't get to at his age. It would be good for him."

"But he is too young," Mom said.

"When I took you rafting, you didn't think you were too young," Grandpa responded.

"Dad, I was fourteen," she said.

"Yes, and I would have taken you when you was younger, but your mom said no. Do you remember how sad you felt, when your mom said no to you that time?" he asked.

"Yes, I do remember," pausing for a moment of reflection, then she finally said, "Okay, he can go, but you will have to make sure it is with a company who has a good reputation with all the safety equipment and their best river guide," Mom told him.

"No problem, we will be going with a group of boys . . . consisting about the same age as Adam, and their parents. The man who is arranging the trip, Andy, has done this every year for several years. He knows what to do, so everything will go smoothly," Grandpa assured her.

"When are you planning on going?" she questioned.

"First week of June or last week of May, whenever they first open for the season," he said.

"Isn't that a little early? The spring runoffs from the ice pack will make the river ice cold," she asked.

"Yes, but we will have wetsuits. Besides we aren't going swimming," Grandpa explained.

Famous last words.

Andy made all the arrangements for the last week of May. Mom was a little apprehensive, making Grandpa and me perform endless promises concerning clothes, taking no chances, watching me every minute, life vests, testing the raft for soundness, interviewing the guide, and on and on and on until we had agreed to a long list of commitments. Finally, we drove away, heading to the high mountain town to begin the journey down the mighty Arkansas River.

Upon arriving at the Rafting Company location, Grandpa went to try to check in with the counter person. He found out the Rafting Company had overbooked and was borrowing some additional rafts from another company. There was a lot of activity, with much confusion and disarray. They had run out of wet suits, so Grandpa volunteered for us to go without. Because of the mix-up, Andy's group was divided, putting us in a different raft. Due to the overbooking, there weren't enough river guides. This meant finding additional river guides.

In all of this scurrying around, Grandpa told the counter person we were with Andy's group. Unfortunately, the counter person thought we were asking to be in the raft that had an Andy as the river guide, not Andy, our group's leader. It was later determined Andy the river guide had only been down the river one time as a guide, but not in the section we were going that day. This was to be his maiden voyage, which meant he had little or no experience before on this river.

While waiting for the additional raft to arrive, Grandpa's friend Andy and his group had already departed down the river. We were the last raft to enter the river after going through all the equipment and gear checks. The water was so cold, freezing. Our raft had nine of us in the raft—Andy, who steered the raft using the rudder, and four of us on each side doing the paddling. Moving along, we tested rowing procedures before our first small rapid. After conquering the first rapid, we felt pretty good about ourselves. I looked at Grandpa, smiling, so happy to be doing this trip on the river in the beautiful wilderness with him, totally unaware of what was about to happen.

The next set of rapids were a little more intense, which got our blood pumping and hearts racing as we paddled, trying to avoid any rocks or entanglements. "This is fun!" I remember telling Grandpa.

Andy then gave us some instructions about the rapids coming up. They were a series of white-water rapids that required heavy paddling to get through them. He explained, "You have to follow a precise line on the river or we could be in trouble. There is a series of four turns, one right after another. As we go through this section, each in turn will become more powerful and violent, creating faster water around large boulders, forcing the narrowing of the channel. Due to the early runoff, the river is higher, creating a fifth rapid and making it a very difficult procedure to perform." Andy then told us he hadn't done this part of the river before, which made it critical to follow his instructions exactly in order to maneuver the raft into the correct channel lanes.

Grandpa whispered to me, "This can't be good."

The first rapid went well; we were lined up in the correct channel. However, on the second one, we were turned a little and didn't hit it straight on. This created a gripping effect on the raft and turned it sideways. Andy couldn't get it turned in time for the third rapid, so we hit it broadside. The raft dipped way down on the front side, sending the people of the high side toward the center of the raft. Of course, all of us were screaming. We did make it out of the third encounter in one piece, except for Andy. I looked back and he was gone. Nobody was steering the raft.

Grandpa frantically reached for the rudder, trying to guide us into a better lane for the fourth rapid, but not in time. We hit it facing backward, with it turning to the side. Our raft smashed a rock, spinning the raft, hit another rock, dipping down then bouncing high in the air. Back and forth we went like a ball in a pinball machine. Grandpa was flung high over the top of the raft, bouncing against the opposite side and creating a trampoline effect on the raft, causing everyone on the one side to fly up four to six feet into the air as the raft dipped down, forcing them all outside of the raft. Two of us managed to hit in the center of the raft, while Grandpa was only in halfway, with his head and arms in the river. I grabbed his legs so he wouldn't fall out. All of the other passengers were in the freezing water, zipping past us yelling. Andy was still nowhere to be found.

The paddles were all gone, except for one and the attached rudder. We were totally out of control, just praying we didn't drown through the disastrous rapid. Somehow, the three of us managed to get past the last turn, only to see the new, fifth rapid right before us, coming up fast.

Grandpa took the rudder while I tried to paddle from the front of the raft. Luckily, we were able to find the right lane, allowing us to pass without any further mishaps.

When we reached calmer water, we searched for the other members of the raft. They were strung out along the edge in shallow water. After pulling them in one by one, Grandpa checked their status. Besides being shaken up, there were only a few bruises and very cold extremities. As we drifted along, we kept searching, but still no sign of Andy.

We continued down the river toward our pickup point, mostly licking our wounds. All of us soaked, exhausted, and cold. By the time we reached the landing area, we'd had enough of river-rafting.

Grandpa, being true to his character, upon safely stepping on land, turned to me and said, "Hey, that was fun; let's do it again!"

I gave him a pained look. Later, we found out Andy had been picked up by another raft from a different company.

Grandpa was right. It was a fun trip—now, looking back on the adventure. It actually was an experience of a lifetime, just as Grandpa said it would be. We never did tell Mom the whole truth about the trip. If she had known, I would never have been able to go on any more trips with Grandpa.

Grandpa and the Two Sticks

One of my favorite memories of Grandpa was when we went to his house for a family gathering. My favorite cousin, Troy, and I were playing together. We weren't very old, maybe five or six. While playing in Grandpa's backyard, I had found an old stick from a tree, on the ground. Being a boy, I started hitting everything with it. It looked like it was fun to Troy, which made him jealous because he didn't have a stick. He asked me if he could play with the stick too. Naturally, I didn't want to share. Grandpa was watching and decided to go find a stick for Troy to solve the problem.

After giving us the two sticks, Grandpa went inside the house. We hit everything in sight, having a great old time. Before long, we decided to have a sword fight. The swinging was very tame at first, but then . . . I accidently hit Troy extra hard on the arm. He gave me a look of anger and then swung harder, hitting me on the arm. Of course, I retaliated, and the duel was on. We beat the heck out of each other. Both us were yelling, swinging with all our might. Blood was everywhere. Both of us had cuts on our heads, arms, legs, stomach, and shoulders. Our parents came running out of the house in a panic. After separating us, my dad asked what had happened.

I told him, "I had found a stick, and since Troy didn't have one, Grandpa made one for him."

As all were looking at Grandpa, Dad asked, "Then what?"

"Grandpa went inside, and we decided to have a sword fight," I said.

Dad turned to Grandpa and questioned, "You gave two little boys each a stick, and then you walked away? What were you thinking? You knew what would happen."

"Well, the one boy had a stick, and the other didn't, so I made one for the other boy to make it even. Then I told them to go hit something. And they did . . ." Grandpa said.

Oh Grandpa, Troy and I still laugh when we talk about that day.

Not Enough Time to Talk

Grandpa lived in Texas. We would drive down every year to visit him, usually in the winter, at the time when the citrus fruit was in season. Grandpa had several grapefruit and orange trees. It was wonderful to return home with a big box of fresh fruit each year. Grandpa would invite us to sit down and visit with him, but since it was our family vacation our time was always filled out, doing activities in the warm Texas sun, giving us a break from the cold Idaho winter days.

Grandpa got up early every morning, preparing to be at work by eight a.m. sharp. For years, Grandpa would follow the same routine; even after he retired, his schedule didn't change much: five a.m. up, treadmill fifteen to thirty minutes, check news, breakfast at seven. Then he would go through his itemized to-do list: check the yard, the trees, the garden, and exterior house each day. After his visual checks, he'd work in the garage, fixing, sharpening, and designing things.

Grandpa would always ask me to help whenever we were in town, to keep him company while he tinkered with things. He just wanted to talk. I would only stay a few minutes, find an excuse, and then head out the door. It wasn't that I didn't like to talk with Grandpa, because I did, but I just had other things to do, being young.

Grandpa was never ill, always available to help anyone in the family. He had no real hobbies, just helping his family.

As years passed, I pretty much stopped traveling to Texas, due to other priorities in my life. When I went to college, Grandpa would phone and send me cards on a regular basis, always including a two-dollar bill! It was interesting; I never quite had the time to have a long conversation with Grandpa on the phone or in person. I was always in a hurry, trying to be somewhere else.

When I bought my first house, Grandpa came to help me finish the basement. While there, he never asked for anything except to spend some time with me while he worked on my house. The problem was I had a new job and couldn't spare any extra time. He understood.

One winter, Grandpa braved the winter weather and drove up to Idaho to bring us some citrus fruit. He said it was because he knew how much I'd loved his grapefruit in my younger years in Texas. His stay wasn't long; we were so busy. I couldn't take time off. How could I? A lot of time just wasn't available at the moment. I had children's events, holiday preparations, and a tough work schedule, but I promised to come down to visit him in Texas soon. I felt a little guilty, but what could I do? I talked to my spouse and decided to plan a trip next year to Texas.

Two years went by. Grandpa was now in his late seventies. I got a call from him one day, just to say hello. We talked for a few minutes, about his trees, his home, and my children. He was having trouble remembering some of the details, but I passed it off as old age. When I told him we would be down there the next summer, he seemed very happy. Four hours later, I received a telephone call that Grandpa was in the hospital with internal bleeding, something to with his brain stem. I jumped on an airplane arriving in Texas at 8:30 p.m. But it was too late. Grandpa had died at 6:30.

At the funeral, many talked of his life and what he had accomplished. I never knew he had done so much. Reflecting back, I realized how little I knew about Grandpa. Through all those years, we had talked about nothing profound, just basic, nice greetings, with normal, surface conversation, nothing of substance. I was always too busy, in a hurry to get out of the house and join my friends or other activities. Now I have the time, but Grandpa doesn't.

In the years since Grandpa's death, I have discovered much about him that I didn't know. Many questions have filled my mind concerning Grandpa. It's ironic, because now I want to talk to him and I can't.

If only . . .

My Annual Trip with Grandpa

Each year, Grandpa would take me for a summer trip. I so enjoyed those trips, seeing various locations, their histories, museums, and interesting places to explore. The time driving in the car, playing games, chatting about everything going on in my life was great. At hotels, we would play at the swimming pool and other youth-related facilities. Eating was always delightful, because I could get anything I wanted. I would eat so much, especially desert.

The one trip that meant so much to me was when we went to Kentucky to a horse festival. Grandpa knew some of the owners, so he got permission to take me to see all of the horses in the stables. It was fantastic. It was a young girl's dream. They were so beautiful; it was so much fun, and I love horses. Knowing this, Grandpa had arranged for me to ride a beautiful black horse, which was the spitting image of Black Beauty. I was so excited. I had just finished reading the Black Beauty series. Sitting on that horse, allowed me to imagine myself being the heroine in the book. When I got back home, I couldn't wait to tell all my friends. They were so jealous. Grandpa made me so happy on that trip. He was so awesome.

Staying at Grandpa's

When my parents would plan one of their getaways, they would expect us to stay at a family member's home. Each time, Mom would ask us where we would want to stay, we would plead to go to Grandpa and Grandma's house. We had fun at PaPa's, because each day he would have something for us to do—play tennis, miniature golf, swimming, a trip to the zoo, or having fun playing silly games. Grandpa loved babysitting us. Even driving to the park was a major event.

"Where do I turn right or left?" he would ask us.

"Turn left," we would say.

"Turn left, right?" he would respond.

"Right!"

Then of course, he would turn right.

"No! No! No!" we would say.

"You said right, right?" he would ask.

"No, we said left!" we told him.

"You said, left, right?" he questioned.

"Yes," we agreed.

"See, you said right again."

This would go on and on with all of us laughing, constantly turning in the wrong direction. Of course, we loved it too, because we never knew what we were going to do next. But most of all, Grandpa loved us, and we loved him.

Grandpa Sleeping in His Chair

My cousin Johnny loved to play tricks on people. One day, we decided to do something to Grandpa. Each third Sunday of the month, our family would go to Grandpa and Grandma's house for dinner. Following the big meal, Grandpa would go sit down in his recliner to watch the game. After approximately fifteen to thirty minutes, Grandpa would be sound asleep. Grandpa didn't just sleep, he snored. The noise was so loud, I swear the ground would be shaking.

Grandma, hearing him would come into the room, muttering, "My Lord," and turn off the TV.

Grandpa would wake up yelling and utter his famous words, "Hey, I was watching that!" It didn't matter how deep asleep he was, if someone turned off the TV, he would always wake up.

Cousin Johnny suggested we put something in Grandpa's mouth while he was sleeping. Johnny thought it would be so funny. The next time Grandpa fell asleep, we snuck up and put a marshmallow is his mouth, then ran as fast as we could, hiding so he wouldn't see us. He woke up wondering what the heck was going on.

Grandpa went around the house asking everyone how he got a marshmallow in his mouth. Grandma chuckling said, "You probably was sleepwalking and found the marshmallow, then put in there yourself."

He scratched his head and went back to watch the game, quickly falling asleep again. Johnny looked at me and said, "Let's do it again. Poor Grandpa, he got things like gumdrops, red hots, crackers, and various other food items."

Each time, Grandma told him he was sleepwalking, but she knew it was us. The extremely hot pepper was the one that ended it all. Grandpa came out of the chair screaming, grabbing his throat, running around—we thought we had killed him.

Grandma pulled us aside and told us no more. I don't think Grandpa ever found out it was us, but I suspect he knew and just pretended to not know.

Hunting with Grandpa

I was about seven, eight years old when Grandpa let me go bird hunting with him. Since we didn't use dogs, he explained it was my job to go fetch the birds after he would shoot them.

He showed me how to mark with my eyes against an object in the distance and align it, so I knew exactly where the bird fell, and then walk there to easily find the bird. It was fun; it gave me a sense of being grown up because I was with the men, hunting. Wow! Grandpa kept me busy, because he was a very good shot. The doves were plentiful that day. I was looking forward to our family cook fest with the doves.

It wasn't long before Grandpa had his daily limit of doves. My great-uncle Albert, along with his son Mark, had gone over to another spot around the bend. Grandpa told me to stay right by the truck while he walked over to help Uncle Albert and Mark.

While he was gone, the game warden drove up and asked if I was alone. I told him no, my Grandpa and Uncle Albert were around the bend.

Bang! Bang! Bang! Several shots rang out over by Grandpa, Mark, and Uncle Albert.

"It sounds like they are having some good luck today," the game warden stated.

Beaming with pride, I told him, "Yes, in fact, Grandpa has already got his limit and is over there helping Uncle Albert get more."

"Really? I think I will just wait here and see what Grandpa comes back with," the warden said.

Bang! Bang! Bang! We hear more shooting. Then Uncle Albert and Mark come around the bend carrying a vest full of birds.

Trying to be helpful, I pointed to them and told the game warden, "It looks like they have a lot of extra birds."

After counting their birds, the game warden discovered each had a few birds over the limit and began to write them a two-hundred-dollar ticket. Just then Grandpa came around the corner with birds in his hand, upon seeing the game warden he quickly dropped them before the warden saw them.

Noticing Grandpa drop the birds, I ran over to fetch them. As my Grandpa arrived at the truck, the warden asked him how many birds he had. Pointing to ones in the truck, he said, "I got my limit right there."

Being proud of my Grandpa's hunting skills, I arrived holding the extra birds and exclaimed, "Don't forget these, Grandpa. I saw where you dropped them, and so we wouldn't accidentally leave them here."

"Thanks, son," he whispered.

"Yes, thanks, son," the game warden said, smiling while looking at Grandpa.

"I am sure glad you brought your grandson today," the game warden said to Grandpa.

The experience has been told and retold at all the family gatherings. Maybe it was not funny at the time, but it became a cherished memory for years afterward.

Another Hunting Experience with Grandpa

Ever' so often, Grandpa and my great-uncle Bill used to go quail hunting in the desert. They would drive on the dirt back roads near dry river bottoms looking for likely spots to hunt, listening for the warning calls from the quail. When they found a potential spot, they would start walking, working their way up the two sides of the draw, trying to flush out a covey of quail. Hunting in the desert landscape allowed a person to experience the view of beautiful, wide-open spaces, not hindered by trees and heavy underbrush. You still had to be careful, because the harsh terrain of rock, boulder, and sand was covered with cactus, spiky brush, or prickly trees and could present some hazardous dangers.

Ever' so often, Grandpa would take me along. Those were treasured times. We would start early in the morning before the sun was up and not return until late evening. They would bring hotdogs to roast, with chips and soda pop. We would be there the whole day. I was too young to carry a gun, so my responsibility was to walk down the draw and try to scare the quail toward Grandpa and Uncle Bill. But sometimes, Grandpa would want me to walk behind him as he showed me various plants and unique items pertaining to the desert.

Grandpa would say, "The secret of understanding the desert is learning how to listen to it."

About midmorning as we were coming down a hill, Grandpa stopped and pointed to a group of mesquite trees. "Listen, do you hear the chatter?" he softly said.

Straining with all my might, I listened. There was no wind just silence. Then, I heard it. A very soft, barely audible . . . it was the single cluck of a male quail. We casually moved toward the trees. When we were about thirty feet from the tree, all heck broke loose—the whole tree exploded with quail. There must have been a hundred of them flying in all directions. I fell over from the sudden surprise. It was like turning the key on a jack-in-the-box, anticipating the release, but still shocked when it finally happened. Grandpa was also shocked, but he did manage to get off all three of his shots. Two right away and one a little later, leaving him with an empty gun. He hit three birds. It was great.

I went and picked up the first two and started looking for the third one behind the brush. For some reason, Grandpa had decided to follow me as I was looking for the third bird. Then I spotted it in a flat brush about twenty feet away. I started to go to get it when Grandpa suddenly grabbed my arm. Pointing right in the middle of the brush, there sat a coiled rattlesnake. The quail had dropped down into the middle of the coil of the rattlesnake.

What are the chances of that happening?

After studying the snake closely, Grandpa determined it was asleep.

As we cautiously approached the snake, we realized there was no way of getting the quail without disturbing the rattlesnake. Grandpa thought if we threw a rock near it to wake it up, it would probably just move away. I backed up. Grandpa found a large-sized rock and threw it, aiming near the snake. Unfortunately, the rock glanced off a bush and landed right on top of the snake's head. That snake shot up in the air furious, looking around for what had hit him. It saw Grandpa and started for him, moving fast. It was mad, and Grandpa was his intended target.

Grandpa tried to cock his gun, but he forgot he hadn't reloaded or put new shells in it. The snake was upon him, trying to attack Grandpa! The rattlesnake didn't even take the time to coil—it went straight for his feet.

While trying to avoid the deadly strikes, he took off running with the rattlesnake hot on his trail. Screaming, Grandpa ran over rocks, around trees, and through bushes, to no avail. That snake was bound and determined to get Grandpa. Grandpa would lift each leg in turn, yelling like a crazy man trying to dodge the constant striking of the snake, while at the same time trying to put a shell into the gun. After dropping two shells on the ground in the scramble, he finally got a shell into the gun, but in his panic it misloaded and jammed the gun.

By this time, Uncle Bill had come running around the corner after hearing all the commotion and was watching the whole process. Now, for an obvious reason, he thought it was funny and started to laugh, watching Grandpa. The chase was continuing, with Grandpa desperately pleading with Uncle Bill to shoot it. This dance must have lasted five to ten minutes before Uncle Bill was able to overcome his laughter and shoot the snake.

Chuckling, Uncle Bill told me, "If your grandpa had been blessed with an Indian heritage, they would have called him Dances with Rattlesnake."

In tribute, Grandpa had the snake's head mounted into a paperweight. As family and friends would come to visit, and noticing the rattlesnake's head in the clear-plastic container with its fangs showing, Grandpa would always have a great story to tell. And what makes it nice, I also have the memory to share.

Grandpa's Big Heart

One time, I was staying at Grandpa's in Colorado. The weather was extremely cold that day. All of the TV stations and radio stations were predicting a heavy snowfall for the area. Grandpa said we better stock up on some food at the store, since we didn't know if we'd be able to get out of the neighborhood once the storm hit.

Grandpa lived in the small town of Castle Rock, Colorado. Castle Rock was in between Denver and Colorado Springs. It would often get heavy snow, because it had a little higher elevation. After going to the store and loading up with our basic supplies that we would need for the next few days, Grandpa decided to stop at the Taco Bell to buy some dinner for us before we went home. It had already started to snow heavily. While eating in the dining area, two highway patrol troopers came in talking to each other and said that the road had now been closed between Castle Rock and Colorado Springs, due to the hostile storms.

It was not uncommon to have multiple accidents on that stretch of road right before Monument Pass. It was a wide-open area where the wind would come whipping through there, right off the mountaintops, blowing heavy snow and ice. The roads would freeze, leaving a dangerous sheet of ice on those roads. Grandpa told me he wasn't surprised they'd closed the road.

A few moments later, after getting off his radio, one of the troopers said to his partner they had better go, because they needed to shut down the road going back to Denver at Surrey Ridge Pass, because there was a multiple-car accident there. Grandpa looked at me and said, "Well it looks like we are not going to leave the city until this blizzard is done; they have closed the road in both directions." After the troopers left, Grandpa saw a woman sitting by herself, noticeably very upset, as if she was getting ready to cry.

Grandpa went over to talk to her and asked her what was wrong. She said, "I don't know what I'm going to do. I can't go back to Denver, and my home is in Colorado Springs. I don't have any money with me, and I have no place to stay here."

Grandpa, recognizing her dilemma, invited her to come stay with us until the storm passed and the roads reopened. Expressing her gratitude, she accepted the offer and followed us to Grandpa and Grandma's house. Grandma was used to having Grandpa bring home people in need. He was always trying to help people who were stressed and, depending on the circumstances, take them home for either a meal or for shelter.

The storm ended up lasting for two days before they could open up the road. During that time, we got to know this nice lady and all the things happening in her life. She had been struggling with many pressures, and Grandpa had a chance to help her by talking to her, encouraging her, providing her with sound advice and suggestions. She was so thankful for that storm, because it allowed her to meet Grandpa. It turned out he was just who and what she needed at that time in her life.

Even though I was young, I never will forget the kindness Grandpa showed to her. I may never know how much of a lasting effect it had on the woman, but I do know the effect it had on me. For my whole life, I have tried to help others to lift their burdens, to encourage, strengthen, and maybe bring a little happiness into their lives. Any time I have a chance to help someone, I think of Grandpa and what he did for that lady that time during the storm. I realize he could've left her there that night at Taco Bell and continued on with his life, not wanting to be involved, but he chose instead to extend a helping hand to someone who was in need. It never ceases to amaze me how many times he made himself available to strangers.

His words of counsel to me still remain in my mind:

"Look for opportunities to help others, and I promise good things will happen in to you in your own life."

Grandpa always seemed to have a brighter smile. His footsteps were more certain. Grandpa had an aura about him of contentment and satisfaction. He believed one cannot participate in helping others without experiencing a rich blessing for oneself.

I have tried to follow that wise counsel, and whenever I do, my life is made better.

Grandpa's Pancakes

Grandpa used to make the very best pancakes. It was a big production at Grandpa's house when he made his famous banana pancakes. We would all anxiously waited to bite into those smooth, wonderful pancakes. Each time, when he would exclaim, "It's time for Grandpa's pancakes!" I would get so excited. Grandpa would only let me cut the bananas and smash them in preparation to be added to the other ingredients. After he added all his secret mixture, he would put it in a big bowl and start stirring, them while the griddle was warming up. I don't know what else he put in those pancakes, but they were sure good.

My four brothers and sister would sit at the table, just waiting. Grandpa would pour out the pancakes onto the griddle in large portions. When Mom made pancakes, they were only about four maybe five inches wide. But with Grandpa, his would always be twelve to fourteen inches, HUGE. Then he would tease my brothers, "I don't know if you can eat these—they are pretty big. You guys are awful small. I think they're too big for you."

Of course, my brothers would respond, "We can eat them, Grandpa!" speaking with their eyes and not their stomachs.

Then Grandpa would say, "Well, you know your dad has the record of thirty-four pancakes at one sitting."

In their minds, the challenge was on: How many pancakes could they eat at one time?

Finally, the pancakes were ready. We would dive in with everything we had. B, but before we would start, Grandpa always had me stand up and take a bow for helping to prepare the pancakes. He made me feel important, as I was a part of that great time.

Five, maybe six, is all we usually ever ate. They tasted so good—my mouth still waters today, thinking about those banana pancakes made by Grandpa. I don't think any of us exceeded more than ten to twelve pancakes at one time. My dad told me that the one time he did eat those thirty-four pancakes, but it happened after he hadn't eaten for a day, coming back from a camping trip in the mountains. He said he was a teenager, seventeen or eighteen, who was terribly hungry. I never got Grandpa's recipe, and to this day, that is one thing I'll always regret.

Midnight Walks with Grandpa

Camping was a big tradition in our family. Each summer, we would take at least a week to go camping in the mountains. It was an escape from the heat and the mundane things of everyday life. The whole experience for me as a child was pure joy. Climbing, fishing, exploring, roughing it, and seeing the true images of nature. Being with Grandpa, Dad, and my siblings gave us the opportunity to forge a family bond, creating memories that could never have been gotten any other way. Sitting around the fire, roasting marshmallows, and making s'mores . . . what an experience.

I vividly recall each of us having the heavy smell of insect spray while covered in dirt from head to toe. The long-remembered part of the camping experience was coming home with inspect-spray-soaked clothes, smelling like smoke from being near the fire.

Grandpa would always tell us scary stories by the light of the fire. He would fill our young minds with wondrous images of ghosts, vicious animals, crazy people, and hidden dangers. Yet, at the same time, he would tell us of heartwarming stories of our ancestors, family members, and friends.

Grandpa knew a lot about the woods, trees, flowers, and wild animals. He would show me different signs made by different animals and the time frame when they were there. During each camping trip, Grandpa would plan a midnight hike. You had to be at a certain age before you could go. Each of us could hardly wait until that magic age of eight. For then, we could qualify to go on the midnight hike with Grandpa.

On the special day for the hike, we would go to bed early, so we wouldn't be too tired to go. Grandpa would check all our gear before we went to bed, making sure we had flashlights, a snack, water, and "an alert mind," as he would say. He would wake us up 11:50 p.m. However, most of us were still awake, because, in anticipation of going on the hike, we couldn't sleep. As we marched out of camp, we would wave back to our family members, for we were going on this great venture into the wilderness. After a few yards away, Grandpa would stop, then have us look back at the campfire so we could get our bearings.

During the hike, Grandpa would have us stand still and listen to the night sounds of the forest, to try to identify each noise. We would pause to look at the stars. Being away from city lights allowed the darkness to be more pronounced, creating a deeper contrast of the stars; they appeared brighter, more plentiful, and beautiful. He would point out different constellations and tell the stories about each one. Of course, he would add in a few things that scared us, and then he would laugh so we knew he was only teasing us.

The midnight hike usually only lasted for about forty-five minutes to an hour, but during that time, our minds were filled with wonderment, and our spirits were uplifted and fed with a real love of nature. We grew closer to Grandpa and shared some great feelings with him.

As we moved back toward camp, he would have us work on our stealth maneuvers, trying to see how close we could get to the camp before someone heard us. Young preteen boys are not very stealthy. We never got close before they knew we were there. Still, our parents would play along, enjoying the excitement that was in our young minds.

I have tried to do midnight hikes with my own children, and it is enjoyable, but it is not the same without Grandpa.

The Forest of Grandchildren

The small section of land around Grandpa's house had an area not being used for any particular purpose. Grandpa decided it would be a good place to plant and grow some trees of various types. Mostly, he said he wanted fruit or nut-bearing trees. While pondering the right trees to plant, Grandpa had an idea come to him.

At the next big family gathering, Grandpa told us he was going to name each tree he planted with the name of one of his grandchildren. The grandchildren would get to choose the tree type, and when we came over, Grandpa and the child would plant it together.

After planting a named tree, Grandpa would make an engraved wooden sign to be placed in front of the tree for all to see the grandchild's name. So upon visiting, each child would see his or her tree. This way, through the years, the child could see the progress as the tree grew.

We were all excited about having our own tree. I picked a pear tree, because it was my favorite fruit. Each year, we would time our visits so I could pick some pears from my tree. I don't know how they tasted to everyone else, but they were the sweetest pears ever to me.

As the years passed, the orchard of trees grew both in size and in numbers as new grandchildren were added to the family. Each year, Grandpa would send us all boxes filled with fruits and different nuts gathered from the Forest of Grandchildren as Grandpa called the orchard. He would always put a note in the box telling from which trees the tasty edibles came. As we ate the various provisions, we would acknowledge the sibling from whose tree came the fruit.

Grandpa took great pleasure in talking about and showing his Forest of Grandchildren. One of his favorite sayings, which we all enjoyed was, "My grandchildren are a bunch of fruits and nuts."

Many years later, after Grandpa passed on, the land was sold. All of us gathered the wooden signs from in front of our trees, to save in remembrance of Grandpa. Yet even today, when I go back by the old farm, I still look for my tree, which produced such sweet pears.

Grandpa and the Penny

Grandpa was a frugal individual. He would clip coupons and check store discounts. Every Wednesday, when the coupons came out in the newspaper, he would schedule his trips to the stores according to which had what items on sale, especially if he had a coupon for the items.

He would say, "Let's go to Safeway, because they have a sale on milk (twenty-five cents less a gallon); then we can go to Food City to pick some hamburger meat (fifty cents less a pound), and then we will stop by Neb's Market to use the coupons for bread."

He was faithful each week, running from store to store to save a few dollars here and there. He would always say, "I lived through the Depression, and it was horrible. It is important you save everything and use as little as possible."

One time, I took Grandpa to the store to buy some items for his house. As we were walking in the parking lot, heading for the store, Grandpa saw a penny on the ground.

Pointing to the penny, he said, "Pick it up; we might need it."

Being a self-conscious teenager of sixteen, I said, "Grandpa, it is only a penny; I don't want to pick it up," thinking all the time, I don't want to pick it up; what if someone saw me? How embarrassing that would be. After all it's only a penny.

Grandpa wouldn't move, keeping with the premise of we might need it. Finally, after checking to make sure nobody was watching, I gave in and picked it up. Of course, at the checkout counter, the price came to $33.01. Grandpa looked at me knowingly as I pulled out the penny we'd found in the parking lot.

He just said, "See?"

Ever since that experience with Grandpa, I never walk by a coin on the ground. It always reminds me of Grandpa and that day. I am happy to say that, many times, the coins I have found have been just the right amount I needed when paying for products. Grandpa was a wise man.

Driving with Grandpa in Swamp Pig

Grandpa lived in Louisiana Cajun country. Whenever we went to Grandpa's, he would take me for a ride in his Swamp Pig. Actually, it was a CJ5 Jeep with big, oversized tires. He had it decked out with a string of lights across the top, so if it got dark, you could see in any direction for several yards. It was a soft-top, which he took off if the weather was good. He had a large winch in front to pull us out of trouble whenever we got stuck. The Swamp Pig could go through anything. We bounced around on all the back roads, through swamps and mud where only a few would be able to go.

Grandpa took me to the best fishing places in the world. We would fish all day and never see another soul. He taught me how to find the right spots on the river, where the brown water meets the clear, and which bait, lures, and gear to use.

He would tell me, "Debbie, you will make the best wife ever. Not only are you the prettiest girl, but you know how to fish. You will be irresistible to any young man."

I loved his heavy Cajun accent, with the French overtones. His favorite phrase was, "I'm happier than an alligator in a pig farm."

Grandpa was just fun to be with. We talked about everything. He had a straightforward country wisdom, which helped me deal with many things in my life. It was all black or white with Grandpa. If it was right, you did it; if it was wrong, you didn't. I am so thankful I had those times with him in Swamp Pig.

Fishing with Grandpa Bo

The one time I remember the most was when I was lucky enough to get to go fishing with Grandpa Bo near his home in Alabama. He had a friend named Skeeder. Each week, they would spend a day fishing on one of the lakes or rivers near his home. Grandpa Bo had decided to invite me to come with him and Skeeder. It was exciting for me. It would be my first fishing trip.

Skeeder had heard of a remote fishing spot that was supposed to have large bass and catfish. So Grandpa Bo thought it would be a good place to take me for my first time catching fish.

We traveled about an hour in the boat before we reached the desired spot. Skeeder was right; we caught several fish that morning. At lunch time, we went ashore to eat. I was having the time of my life. While on shore, Grandpa Bo found a nest of newborn water moccasin snakes. They were too small to bite you or cause any harm. Skeeder was deathly afraid of snakes, though, and wouldn't have anything to do with them—especially poisonous snakes like water moccasins. Grandpa Bo thought it would be a good idea to use them as bait. Their size was just a little bigger than a worm, but they were much more active.

Returning to fishing, Grandpa put on one of the small snakes and tossed it in the water. *Wham!* He got a strike immediately. For the next several minutes, each time he threw out the line, he would catch a fish. He put one on my line, and the same happened for me. We were having a terrific time catching fish. Skeeder never touched the snakes.

Grandpa saw a spot across the river and suggested to Skeeder he would like to try it. There was some brush, but he felt that it would be a great place to find one of those huge fish Skeeder had heard about.

Grandpa threw his line over the top of some brush into a small, clear channel. Immediately, the line went down, bending the pole almost in half. I was afraid it was going to break.

Grandpa yelled to Skeeder, "This is a big'n!"

It must have been a big fish, because it started to pull the boat around. As the line was passing the brush, something hit the taut line. It was a full-grown water moccasin! The line had disturbed the snake, and it was working its way up the line toward the boat. Now, Grandpa had to decide what to do. He didn't want to lose the fish, nor did he want a ticked-off poisonous snake on his pole.

Grandpa Bo scooted back in the boat, hoping he could shake the snake off the line. But it was coming too fast—instead of knocking it off into the water, it fell into the boat!

Now we had an upset, poisonous snake darting around in the boat, Grandpa Bo was still trying to land what he thought was the biggest fish in his life, and me and Skeeder were screaming in fear for our lives.

In panic, Skeeder starts jumping around in the boat, trying to hit the snake with his pole—*Whap, Whap, Whap*—which just made the snake angrier. Trying to get away from Skeeder's hammering, it sees me and starts after me. Noticing this, Grandpa Bo shoves me into the water just in time, before the snake strikes, while he is still desperately holding the fishing pole with the fish on the line. Since I had a full life vest on, I was safer in the water than in the boat.

By now, Skeeder has lost it. He is screaming at a high, almost girlish pitch, rocking the boat to where it is about to tip over and cause even more pandemonium with him, the snake, and Grandpa Bo. Finally, he loses his balance and falls into the water!

Now it was just Grandpa Bo and the snake in the boat. The snake wanted to get Grandpa Bo, and Grandpa Bo wanted the fish. From one side of the boat to the other, they did the tango, all the while with Grandpa Bo not letting go of the fishing pole. After a few minutes of terror, Grandpa Bo sees me swimming by the boat and tosses the pole to me, telling me to hang onto the pole and not let go of the fish.

We were on the downriver side of the boat, and at that moment, feeling a little slack in the line, the fish decided to make a break for it. The fish took off downriver. Since I couldn't touch bottom, I didn't have any footing. The fish started to pull me with it. Feeling it might have some freedom, the fish started moving fast. And I am holding on for dear life being dragged along!

If a person would have been on the riverbank, it would have been quite a show with Grandpa Bo rolling around in the boat trying to kill or capture the snake without being bit, Skeeder in the water still yelling, and me with my pole in the air being pulled along the river.

Finally, Grandpa Bo was able to hit the snake with the oar, stunning it enough so he could get hold of it and throw it away from the boat. However, he threw it on the side where Skeeder was swimming. Of course, as soon he tossed it into the water,

Skeeder began yelling to get him out and back into the boat. After hauling Skeeder into the boat, they start looking for me. By now, I am a quarter of a mile away and still moving fast, being dragged by the fish.

Grandpa Bo gets the motor started to come and get me. After a few minutes, he pulls alongside of me and reaches for the fishing pole. Once he secured the pole, he and Skeeder pull me into the boat. Unfortunately, the strain on the fishing line was too much, and the line broke at that moment.

Grandpa dejectedly said, "No fish. No snake. No proof."

"Oh yeah? What about my additional white hair?" Skeeder cried.

It was a great time fishing with Grandpa Bo.

Hands in the Cement

At Grandpa and Grandma's house, they had a long walkway in their back yard. When Grandpa was planning the walkway, he had a thought come to him while he was visiting a nursery. He saw a block of cement with names on it. The names were put there by children when the cement was wet.

So he bought a form to make different block designs and cement. At his home he poured the cement in the block forms and let his children put their handprints in the wet cement, along with his and Grandma's. Then he wrote their names in the cement below the handprints. He made one block for each of his five children. There was a different design for each of his children. As each of his children got married, he would add the spouse's name to the family walkway, using the appropriate design to create a family pattern.

Through the years, Grandpa would add new blocks for each new grandchild, each placing our handprints along with the grandparents'. The walkway grew to over twenty-five block-forms of grandchildren. Another trail broke off the original when the great-grandchildren started to come into the family. Each new block made in the proper design of the family crest.

Whenever we visited, each of us would go stand on our blocks and put our hands over our small prints, comparing how much we had grown. Then we would place our hands in the prints of Grandma and Grandpa.

After Grandpa and Grandma died, we all took our blocks to remind us of them. Even today, I will place my hand in their handprints to feel the connection. It brings back all the good memories I experienced at their home as a child. Even though my children don't remember them too well, the two oldest ones have their own blocks with their great-grandparents' handprints in them.

Creating special memories requires time and ample opportunity to share something unusual that will stay in the grandchild's mind. All have a need to feel important, loved, and accepted, and grandfathers have a unique chance to affect the grandchildren's lives in a great way. Rarely does planning an event result in a cherished memory; usually it just happens, at odd times, unexpectedly. If you put in the effort, an extraordinary connection is formed between grandfather and grandchild, firmly planting the seed of an unforgettable occasion to be cherished forever.

Chapter 24

Strong as Metal, Soft as Fleece

The strongest grandpa is not afraid of lightning storms, scary movies, the dark, or monsters, but will run in terror from the word "Boo!" yelled by a small child.

—Robert Brault

In order to be the rock in the river that the water cannot loosen or wash away, I suggest you seek help from a higher source to guide you through these troubled waters. Don't just rely on the wisdom of the world, for it is flawed and unstable. Don't underestimate the power from above.

It is necessary to develop distinguishing traits to be the best grandfather you can be. Most great leaders throughout history give credit to a higher source beyond themselves. Believe it, don't believe it, it makes no difference; the higher power is there; just like gravity, it does exist. Use it to your advantage.

Throughout history, the attributes that made great leaders great were learned, not inherited, often patterned after positive, male role models introduced into their lives for that reason.

A successful grandfather of today must have two characteristics: one, the strength of metal, and the other, the softness of fleece.

Strong as metal means having the fortitude to meet the responsibilities required of today. If you have this character of metal, you are these things:

resilient	stable	safe	truthful
tough	secure	steady	protective
powerful	solid	sturdy	courageous

Soft as fleece means having the compassion to meet the needs of others. Having the attributes of fleece means you can be described like this:

tender	merciful	empathetic
loving	showing	considerate
charitable	humor	tactful
gentle	kindhearted	
sensitive	caring	

Few men in history have displayed the qualities of both metal and fleece. Some men only develop one or the other. We all have known those kind of men in our lives and in history. But one famous leader was known for having the ability to show both strength and gentleness. He was President Dwight D. Eisenhower. His leadership lasted for almost two decades. Few men have influenced modern American history as he has done. His role when a five-star general in the US Army as the Supreme Allied Commander during one of our darkest times in history affected millions of people throughout the world. The decisions he was forced to make were so heavy, most men would have cracked under the pressure. Eisenhower planned and oversaw the Allied troops through massive assaults and difficult campaigns.

Eisenhower's style of leadership was one of confidence and a highly developed work ethic. It matters not rather it was turned toward a triumphant campaign or a horrible mistake, his leadership always fed those around him with courage and unwavering self-assurance. That defiance against all odds allowed him to stand tall with the weight of the world on his shoulders and boldly make critical decisions. He alone made the decision for D-Day; neither Roosevelt nor Churchill challenged his chosen time and place, despite heavy odds against success. He knew if he made the wrong decision, the war could be lost.

Those who served with him learned to trust in his decisions. His dedication and straightforward manner removed any doubt about his leadership abilities. He inspired those around him to follow his example of high ideals and a heightened sense of duty to accomplish tasks at difficult times. But he maintained an easygoing, friendly attitude and a genuine humility that endeared him to those around him. He never sought fame, attention, or power in his position. His qualities inspired loyalty, affection, and admiration from those who served under him. Ike was known for his ability to listen, understand, and encourage others. He became like a father and mentor to those he led. Very few men in history could have performed with such strength and balance with what was put on his shoulders.

Families need grandpas who show both the strength of metal and the softness of fleece. Someone who is strong and sturdy, a pillar to support others especially in times of trouble, yet who can feel the need for kindness, be sensitive and tenderhearted toward the needs and feelings of others when required.

All of the previous chapters were designed to help you develop these two traits. I realize it isn't easy to just become someone different from who we have been our whole lives. But it can be done with practice.

Chapter 25

The Element of Change

In our youth, confidence concerning our desires, goals, and plans was certain. But through life's trials, it wavers. The older we get, the only sure thing is change. Change is like an old friend, ever present, always there. Life is laced with changes—if you aren't happy with this, then change your attitude.

—Grandpa G

We have all heard the saying, the only two things you can count on are death and taxes. I would like to propose a third element, *change*. The most constant thing in our life is change.

From the beginning to the end of our lives, we must deal with change. Some changes we embrace, while others we resist. There are changes in our lives that are sudden and unforeseen, such as the unexpected passing of a loved one, the loss of a job, illness (temporary or life-changing), a financial loss, divorce, or the loss of a valued possession. But most of the changes take place subtly and slowly.

Burdens and stress are a part of our lives. It doesn't matter who we are—young, old, rich, poor, healthy, or physically challenged—we will have problems placed upon us regardless of our circumstances. We have to deal with them the best we can. However, we must not let them get in the way of what is most important in our lives—those we love.

Often we assume that they must know how much we love them. That is a mistaken assumption. For both your and their well-being, you should let them know.

> *Love that is not expressed is lost, as if it never existed.*
> —Grandpa G

With kindness and sincerity, we must express words of affection, for if we don't, feelings of regret will enter into our lives. No thoughts or feelings must be left unsaid. Nothing should be withheld from our closest relationships, from those who mean the most to us.

Find a way to communicate to your grandchildren, children, and family members. Send a note, e-mail, text, or call—and don't put it off for a better time. Give hugs to your children, grandchildren, spouse, parents, and close friends; say "I love you" to them. It is essential you express your thanks to them for being a part of your life. Move beyond any problems; find solutions, because no problem is more important than the ones you love.

Our lives never sit still, but are always moving forward; Children grow up, friends move away, jobs change, loved ones pass on. How easy it is to take things and others for granted. Then one unexpected day, they're gone from our lives.

The following story was told by a man who lost his wife.

> From the time we were young, my wife and I had planned our life vacation of retirement. We studied places we wanted to visit. We outlined trips around the world to places of history, exciting islands, and religious sites. We were going to learn new hobbies, buy our RV, dance on cruises, and have great adventures. We had an architect design our dream home, which we would build. Our idea was to be near our children and grandchildren to watch them grow up and be a part of their lives.

To accomplish these projects, we knew we would have to sacrifice in our younger years so we could enjoy the fruits of our labors. We cut back in every area of our lives—on vacations, presents, and trips to family. Our house was too small for our family, but the affordable cost allowed us to put aside funds toward our retirement. We penny-pinched everything we could. Our efforts took a lot of hard work, saving for our goals: *Save now, play later.*

Finally, when we reached retirement age, we had an abundance of resources to reap the fruits of our sacrifices. We had obtained our desired goal.

With our dream house built, we began the excitement of putting our long-awaited plan into reality. The first on our list was a cruise to the islands. Our departure date was in April. We were knee-deep in preparations, with much activity. During that time, I noticed my wife, Sarah, was more tired than usual. She started to have an unusual amount of headaches. We went to visit the doctor, because we didn't want her to feel sick on the cruise. After several tests, the results were devastating.

She had a life-threatening illness. For the next few months, more tests, more treatments, and more drugs. In the end, she continued to decline. She passed away a year later.

During her sickness, we lost everything—the house, our savings, and our dreams. All that sacrificing for naught. If I had just known, we could have done so much more when we were younger . . .

The saddest tears are spilled over graves, regretting words unsaid and acts undone.

—Grandpa G

Many times, we are left with feelings of *what if* and *if only*. But it is important to relish life *as* we live it, finding joy in the journey, sharing our love with friends and family, not waiting for some future events to come together, a time that may never come. *One day, each of us will run out of tomorrows.*

This parable is from the Bible, New Testament, King James Version:

> The ground of a certain rich man brought forth plentifully:
>
> And he thought within himself, saying, What shall I do, because I have no room where to bestow my fruits?
>
> And he said, This will I do: I will pull down my barns, and build greater; and there will I bestow all my fruits and goods.
>
> And I will say to my soul, Soul, thou hast much goods laid up for many years; take thine ease, eat, drink, and be merry.
>
> But God said unto him, Thou fool, this night thy soul shall be required of thee: then whose shall those things be, which thou hast provided?
>
> So is he that layeth up treasure for himself, and is not rich toward God.
>
> —Luke 12:16–21

Our time here on earth is measured in seconds, minutes, hours, days, months, and years, always moving forward, taking us from the past to the present. As the time in our lives moves forward, so will its changes. Some we can control, others we cannot. The ones we can control are the most important. The smallest details in decisions made regarding those who are involved in our lives make the biggest impact in their and our happiness. It requires of us to make good and righteous choices.

This is our one and only chance at mortal life, here and now. The longer we live, the greater is our realization that it is brief. As opportunities come, our time with children and grandchildren is limited, and then it is gone. Maybe the greatest lessons we are to learn in this short time upon the earth are lessons that help us distinguish between what is important and what is not. Moments are precious. Grandfather, you must spend them wisely. Don't look ahead for better times; use the time you have to make good memories for your family. It is important you find joy in *now*.

In the always popular musical play *The Music Man,* the main character issues a warning to us all. Professor Harold Hill says,

> *If you pile up enough tomorrows, then you'll find you've collected a lot of empty yesterdays.*
>
> —Meredith Willson, playwright

Grandpa, you can't create meaningful experiences with your grandchildren for them to recall for the rest of their lives if you don't do something with them today. Children need positive experiences that become lasting memories to have a sense of family connection. This is your time and opportunity to create those memories.

From a grandpa:

> We were going to take our three grandchildren to the state fair. We had been planning for weeks. Our discussions of cotton candy, candy apples, and other delightful treats enticed the minds of our grandchildren. The promise of all sorts of rides on the midway brought a high level of anticipation. Even the opportunity to see all the animals that would be judged for the blue ribbons generated a joy of elation and had to be put on the must-see list.
>
> The day we were scheduled to go to the fair, an important client called for a must-attend, urgent meeting. I was in a dilemma; I had to make a very hard decision. If I took the children to the fair, I could risk losing the client. If I went to the meeting, I would greatly disappoint my grandchildren.
>
> "Go to work, for there will be other fairs, you know," Grandma suggested.
>
> After the phone call and overhearing Grandma and my discussion, the grandchildren were prepared for

disappointment. Seeing this on their sweet little faces was what prompted my decision.

I then told Grandma, "I will miss the meeting with the client, and it will have to be rescheduled."

"Are you sure? The state fair can wait," she said.

"Yes, I know, but childhood doesn't," I responded.

If you have children who are grown and gone, in all likelihood you harbor an occasional pang of regret for the lost opportunities you didn't appreciate or take advantage of during the time you had with your children. Of course, there is no going back, but only forward. Rather than dwelling on the past, we should make the most of today, of the here and now, doing all we can to share sweet experiences in the present, which provide pleasant memories for the future. *The next generation is before you. There is a new opportunity to help, to share, to strengthen, and to love.*

Be aware that the tiny fingerprints that show up on almost every newly cleaned surface, the toys scattered about the house, the piles and piles of dirty laundry to be tackled will disappear all-too-soon, and you will, to your surprise, miss them profoundly.

A grandpa shared his experience with me.

My wife was an immaculate housekeeper. Everything was spotless, clean, and in perfect order. Any disruption to the orderly house created major reactions from her. Before grandchildren were to come to visit, she spent hours childproofing the home. While the children were in the home, the rules would be enforced, without exception.

Then came the diagnosis: she had cancer. For her, the world had been turned upside down. The sobering reality of possible death forced her to reevaluate what really mattered to her in her life. Patterns changed; the house wasn't important, but the children were to her. Spilled milk, cupboards left open, dirty dishes in the sink, accidentally broken items were of less value. What mattered the most was time spent with the children. Those perceived-as-expensive material items now meant nothing; the treasure had changed to her grandchildren and children.

Our lives consist of past, present, and future. Our past history is where we gain knowledge, but it is not where we live. The past is to learn from, but not lived in. The future can be dreamed about or planned for, but likewise, not lived in. It is still unknown and uncertain. We must live in the present, today. Each moment is precious with our children and grandchildren.

We do not know what is around the corner. But I assure you, it will be different from what you imagine. Our lives are in constant motion, a moving target. The only absolute is change. Live for now, not later.

Summary

Life is like a coin—you can only spend it once.
     —Lillian Dickson, founder of the Mustard Seed

I firmly believe that any man's finest hour, the greatest fulfillment of all that he holds dear, is the moment when he has worked his heart out in a good cause and lies exhausted on the field of battle—victorious.
     —Vince Lombardi, longtime coach
     of the Green Bay Packers

As we learn and grow, we become stronger for facing and surviving the trials through which we must pass. Our life here wasn't designed to be easy, but for us to learn, expand, develop new attributes, experience the joys of serving others, and become more refined. So it must be with us as grandfathers. We know that there are times when we will experience heartbreaking sorrow, when we will grieve, and when we are tested to our limits. However, such difficulties allow us to change for the better, to rebuild our lives into a higher level of understanding of what is acceptable to us, our family, and our creator. These experiences will make us something different from what we were, better than we were, more understanding than we were, more empathetic than we were, with stronger family relations than we had before. Our lives can and should be a beacon to those we care most about.

This should be our purpose through which to persevere and endure. It allows us to become more refined as we make our way through sunshine and sorrow. Were it not for the challenges to overcome and problems to solve, we would remain much as we were born, with little or no progress toward our goals. Many can and will go with the wind, but the strongest soar higher when they go against it. There is a poem, beautiful yet wonderfully simple, that expresses these thoughts:

> Good timber does not grow with ease,
> The stronger wind, the stronger trees.
> The further sky, the greater length.
> The more the storm, the more the strength.
> By sun and cold, by rain and snow,
> In trees and men, good timbers grow.
>   —Douglas Malloch, "Good Timber"[7]

Don't look at today's problems or today's successes as the end. They are only temporary. *Legacy is overtime.* Attitudes, morals, deep impressions, and spiritual growth come with the expenditure of time. Teaching, sharing, and strengthening the young minds of our grandchildren in order for them to have foundations on which to build their own character is of the greatest worth. The challenges of the world today require all our resources to be used with the children so they are not influenced by the evils that lead them away from happy, successful lives.

Spending time, listening, and guiding with patience and positive motivation gives them strength. We must be the guardians of virtue, principles, and stability. When times become tough for them, they will have your example to reflect on for encouragement, to empower them in times of need. Helping them to build a strong infrastructure within will allow them to pass on to the next generation solid standards, even after we are long gone. You may be the only anchor for them to depend upon in the future. And hopefully, when they think of

---

7   In Sterling W. Sill, *Making the Most of Yourself,* Salt Lake City, UT: Bookcraft Inc., 1971, 23.

you it will bring a smile remembering your humor, your love, your stories, and your example.

The attributes and characteristics presented in this book, if applied, can magnify your calling and responsibility as a respected, awesome grandfather. I believe there isn't a higher position given to man—be it king, president, or great leader—than the role and responsibility of a husband, father, and grandfather. This is our reason for existence, to fulfill our place in the annals of time, to complete our roles in mankind. Now is our time to perform the tasks we have been sent to do. Procrastination is a luxury we can't afford, for we do not know what is around the corner.

As Grandpa G says, "Death is the master of us all, and he will be calling upon us in the future. For some soon, others later, but he will show up at our door, prepared or not. For most of us, we are in the winter of our lives. The leaves have fallen, the memories are secure, our futures uncertain, but for today, I have children and grandchildren to be held, loved, and served."

Never forget to enjoy the pure fun and pleasure of being a father and grandfather. Laugh, play, and immerse yourself in the wonderment of children. Laugh at yourself . . . and with others.

Here are a few fun thoughts of being a grandfather to enjoy and relate to:

> *A grandfather is someone with silver in his hair and gold in his heart.*
>
> —Unknown Author

> *As smart as Grandpa is, he still acts like he doesn't know who you are on Halloween.*
>
> —Grandpa G

> *My grandfather once told me that there are two kinds of people: those who work and those who take the credit. He told me to try to be in the first group; there is less competition there.*
>
> —Gandi

Grandfathers are good at sitting on the floor to play, but they can be terribly difficult when getting upright again.

—Grandpa G

An important fact to remember: we are not alone. We do have a Father helping us. Think of him in our lives. The following is a delightful story to illustrate the point.

A grandpa overhead his grandson's prayer. The youth had been taught by his grandfather about his beliefs and the importance of prayer. (Again, you never know what they will grasp.)

> Dear God, please take care of my grandpa, my grandma, my daddy, and my mommy, and my sister, and my brother, and my doggy, and me . . . Oh, please take care of yourself, God. If anything happens to you, we're gonna be in a big mess.

The final words come from Grandpa G:

> *I will rest when I am dead. I want to be able to say, "When my time comes, I was all used up, nothing left undone."*